THIS TWISTED LIFE

Author

Tracye D. Bryant

T. Bryant Media Group Inc.

Copyright @2012 by Tracye D. Bryant

Published by T. Bryant Media Group, Inc.
425 Skif Pond Court, College Park, Georgia 30349

Library of Congress Control Number: 2016909559

ISBN 978-0-9976946-0-4

Printed in the United States of America

Cover Design
Pamela Stover
www.pamelastover.com

Melissa thank
you dear, for your love and
support. I pray this story
makes you L.O.L. as you relate
to the characters and their journey!

All the best,

Tracye Bryant

Epigraph

Hebrews 11:1- *Now faith is the substance of things hoped for and the evidence of things not seen.*

I dedicate this book to the loves of my life - my boys Avery and Mason. The two of you are truly my greatest inspiration in life. I continue to thank God for blessing me with two of the most amazing children. Please know that my love for you is endless and that I am so proud of each of you. ~Mommy

Acknowledgements:

I have always been a person who treasured the love and support that I have received over the years from my family and friends. Although words may never be able to express my true feelings of appreciation and gratitude for each of you, I will try my best.

Wilma Walker – My mom, my cheerleader, and my greatest supporter I say thank you. Thank you mom for always allowing me to dream in color no matter how big or how small. Even as an adult, you have continued to encourage all the crazy thoughts and ideas I have come up with over the years. I appreciate the life lessons that you have taught me, and most of all, for showing me how important it is to always keep God first in my life. PS. Thank you for spoiling me...

Thomas Wright – Pop, for years you have stood behind me supporting every big event in my life. I appreciate you for loving me no matter what and never letting anybody question our father-daughter relationship. It is my hope to continue to make you proud and give you something to "brag" about.

Al Bryant – I thank God for you. Our children are the luckiest kids on earth to have such a loving, caring, involved and concerned father in their life. I appreciate you for loving me no matter what.

Kevin Stroud – My "baby" Brother, I love you for always being right beside me, good, bad or otherwise. Growing up, I couldn't have imagined not having you as my sibling. I pray that this book makes you as proud of me as I am of you.

Hazel Hampton – My grandmother, I love and appreciate you more than I let on at times. Through the years, your strength has help guide the way, and for that, I say thank you.

Candice McNeil – My best friend, my sister and my confidant. Words can never truly express my love and appreciation for you. With each day, I thank God for the more than 20 years of friendship that we have shared. Your continuous support, love and encouragement help me to

6

stay focused and for that I say "thank you" and most of all I Love You! Let's make this BIG!

Mike C. Lymon – "Bruh-law" I simply say to you thank you. You have always trusted and believed in me and allowed me to play an intricate part in the many great things you have done in the community and in the lives of those you care about the most. You mean so much to me and I hope that over the years I have shown myself to be half the level of support to you that you have displayed to my family and me. You are an extraordinary person with a heart the size of Mt. Everest; please know that God will continue to bless you and all that you do.

Pastor Dier Hopkins – Pastor Hopkins, you have truly been an inspiration to me. Since the first day I met you, I was blessed by God's directive to connect our spirit. You are a mighty man of God and I truly appreciate all the prayers you did with me personally over the phone during the process of writing this book. I appreciate all the constructive criticisms you provided and the oftentimes push back on the direction of your "favorite" characters. Thank you for your continued prayer and support, and, most of all, for believing in me.

Isis Navies – It is not often that people find such strong influences in their lives and are able to call that person a mentor and a friend. Isis since the first day I met you I have felt the blessings of God on our relationship. Your love, support, words of inspiration and words of wisdom have left a profound impact on my life. I truly consider myself blessed to be able to pick up the phone on any given day and have access to a woman of your caliber with so much heartfelt advice and mentoring direction. Thank you for loving me like one of your own and welcoming me into your family. I know you're smiling as a result of this book and I can't wait until the "day after" conversation we will have soon. Much love to you!

Donna Permell – My "famed" photographer! Your friendship and support over the years has allowed me the opportunity to explore the creativity within me. I love and appreciate you for "just being you" and making sure that I knew you loved me for "just being me". Thank you for always showing the world my beauty through your lens.

7

Rashida Rawls – My AMAZING editor! From the first day I called you and asked you to take a look at this project you jumped right in, no questions asked. I love how you were immediately connected and instantly saw the huge potential in this story and committed to seeing it be successful. Thank you for the countless hours of reading, reviewing and meetings to make sure that it was "perfect!" New York Times, here we come!

Please know that if I left anyone out it was not intentional, just not enough time and space to call everybody's name. But I love you!

Prologue

Sherita sat on the side of the bed with her head hung low. The past 48 hours seemed like a blur. As much as she wanted to believe that she was in the midst of an impossible nightmare, she was quickly reminded that the loss she had experienced was all too real.

"Mom?" Josh knocked lightly on the door.

Without saying a word, she looked up into her son's eyes.

"Mom, can I get you anything?"

"No sweetie, I am fine. Thank you," she said softly.

Josh sat down on the bed next to his mom and gently pulled her body toward his until her head rested on his chest. As she wept lightly, he couldn't help but feel like this was partly his fault. The last thing Josh wanted was to see his Mom crying and in search of answers. As the two sat in silence, the stillness of the room was abruptly interrupted by the phone.

"Hello?" Josh answered.

"Hey Josh, it's me, Alana. How is mom holding up?" she asked with concern. "Ah, we are sitting here now. She seems to be coming along as well as can be expected. Want to talk to her?"

"Yeah, if she's up to it."

Gently wiping tears from her eyes, Sherita takes the phone.

"Hey Lan, sweetie – how are you?" Sherita asked.

"Mom I am fine. The question is - how are you?"

"I am coming along. Just trying to put together the pieces to it all in my head, but I will be fine. When are you coming home?" she asked.

"Um, Daddy bought me a ticket last night and my flight gets in this evening at 7:20. I was calling to ask Josh if he would pick me up from the airport?"

"I am sure your brother will make himself available to pick you up. I will let him know what time. The services have been scheduled for tomorrow morning and I think it would be good for us all to be there to show support."

Alana was a bit taken aback at her mother's calm demeanor over the phone. Perhaps she had already cried as much as she could, but the way she was acting was just out of character for her. As Alana hung up the phone, she couldn't help but feel sad for her mom. The past few weeks had been a tremendous burden it seemed. First, the death of her best friend, and now this. Alana just couldn't imagine what that must be like.

Looking at the clock, it was almost 10:00 a.m., she didn't have much time to run errands, have lunch with Bella and Nehemiah and then take a taxi to LaGuardia International Airport to catch the flight home. The weather in New York was already cool and crisp. As Alana slipped on her coat and scarf, she headed up the street to grab a cup of coffee from a nearby street vendor. Waiting in line, she caught the eye of a handsome stranger. They exchanged pleasant hellos with their eyes, but never spoke. The hustle and bustle of New York City never stopped. Everyone seemed to be in a rush to go nowhere. Heading North on Broadway Street, Alana knew it would take her about 25 minutes or so to make it to the Gray's Papaya Restaurant on 6th Avenue for lunch. However, she had one stop she needed to make at the drug store. As she entered the building, she got this overwhelming sense that she was being watched. Trying not to be paranoid, she quickly shopped for the items she needed and headed to the checkout counter. Turning the corner, she surprisingly runs into the intriguing stranger from the coffee stand earlier.

"Are you following me?" she asked annoyed.

Realizing that his immature attempt to get her attention didn't go as planned; he let out a nervous sigh.

"Um, sorry. Yeah, sort of. You walked away so quickly earlier that I didn't get an opportunity to say something to you," he said.

Alana was leery at this point and not feeling this strange man's feeble attempt to talk to her. She abruptly pushed her way past him.

"Yeah, well, I am not interested. Keep it moving."

Not wanting to startle her any further, he complied with her request and left. Paranoid all the more, Alana paid for her things and rushed out to get to the restaurant. She had to be careful of the creepy people who would approach her at any time and really needed to stay focused. She was shaken by the encounter with the stranger. As she entered the restaurant, she looked flushed.

"Hey Alana. Honey, what's wrong? You look like you just saw a ghost or something," said Nehemiah as he stood to greet her coming in the door.

Visibly shaken by the entire incident, Alana took a deep breath and shared her encounter as she took off her coat. Bella had gone to the restroom and the two waited for her to return before ordering. As she approached her friends, Bella could see that Nehemiah appeared to be comforting Alana, who looked scared.

"What's going on?" she asked.

"Some guy followed Alana into the drug store and tried to talk to her. She is just a bit shaken up."

Instantly concerned for her friend, Bella reacted.

"Oh my God, are you alright?" she asked.

"Yes, I am fine. He went on about his business and it's over. I guess I am just a ball of nerves today anyway knowing that I have to go home this evening and deal with this stuff with my family," Alana said.

"Well honey, you are safe now. So just relax and let's get something to eat," Nehemiah said.

After lunch, the three headed back to the dorm to help Alana finish packing for the trip home. Not wasting any time, Alana knew she would be gone for at least 4 days and only took what she needed for the funeral. The weather in Atlanta was still relatively warm and she had plenty of clothes at home.

"So, Alana, how is your family holding up?" Bella asked.

"You know, I am not sure. The past 12 months have been an interesting twist of events for us and hopefully, this is the end of this whirlwind," she said.

Alana sat on the bed gazing aimlessly out the window as she thought back over the past year and how so much had changed in their lives. Who knew, life really isn't a series of happy endings, and yet there were more surprises still in store.

One year earlier…

Chapter 1

It's Monday morning, and things are hectic in the Coleman household. The house is noisy as 17-year-old Alana contemplates what to wear on the first day of her senior year of high school. Her younger brother 16-year-old Josh is in the bathroom "shaving" a blind hair on his chin. In the background, the television from downstairs in the kitchen is blaring, while the neighbors' dog is barking frantically outside. Alana looks at herself in the mirror, deciding this is sure to be the worst day.

"If only I were already out of high school, I would be working my dream job, making lots of money and traveling the world," she thinks as she playfully spins around and comes face-to-face with clothes strewn everywhere.

"Meanwhile, I am here, frustrated with what to wear on this lousy first day of school."

She sighs.

"Let's GO!"

A strong insistent voice yells to the top of the stairs. Alana begins to rush to finish dressing when she realizes that the finishing touches are in the bathroom with Josh. Banging on the door, she yells, "Josh, can you please come out of the bathroom so that I can get finished. Mom is ready to go!"

"Shut-up," he yells back.

"Oh my God, Josh, I hate you. Mom!"

Sherita yells back.

"LET'S GO! I am going to be late and I do not have time to referee a bathroom battle between the two of you this morning."

Josh gives himself another dose with hot water to the face, checking out his amateur masterpiece of a shave.

"Not bad," he says while admiring himself in the mirror.

He then notices a few nicks that are starting to bleed.

"Ahhh damn," he says in frustration, he looks under the cabinet for a bandage.

The only ones available are the full-size cartoon character band-aid that Alana bought for a project last year. Upset, he throws his hand in the air, as he reaches for the toilet paper – "this will have to do."

Shortly thereafter, Josh emerges from the restroom with spots of toilet paper stuck to his face, where his attempt at shaving has failed miserably.

"There, happy now?" he snarls at his sister, who is waiting impatiently

outside the door.

"Urrgghh," she grunts in anguish.

As Alana rushes into the restroom, Josh scrambles to get dressed. The

phone is ringing off the hook and finally Sherita decides to answer.

"Hello….," "hello!" she yells into the phone.

A familiar male voice on the other end startles her.

"Hey! Good morning, can you hear me OK?"

"Yes, I can hear you now," she answers.

"How are you this morning?"

"I am fine. Just running late! Hold on, let me let you talk to the kids,"

laying the phone on the kitchen counter, she yells toward the ceiling,

"Alana! Your dad's on the phone."

Alana picks up the phone in her room.

"Hi Daddy!"

"Hey sweetheart, how's my girl?"

"I am good, trying to get ready for school."

17

"Yeah, sounds like it, your mother seemed stressed when she answered the phone. What are you and your brother doing and why is it taking so long?"

"Daddy, Josh *was* adopted right?" She asks with a serious look of inquiry on her face.

"What?" he asks with a chuckle.

"I mean, he can't really be a part of this family. He is just weird and aggravating and slow, Daddy," she says with conviction. Smiling in the phone, Tyrone Coleman can't help but love his children.

"Alana, honey, give your brother a break. You know it takes guys a little longer to get the hang of things than girls, and hopefully one day he will grow out of it." "Hmmm… one can only hope Daddy, one can only hope. Alright, well, love you – let me let you talk to the village idiot. I mean the hopeful one."

"OK sweetie, have a great first day!"

"Thanks Daddy, you, too."

"JOSH! DAD!" She yells down the hall.

Digging through a pile of clothes on the floor in his closet in pursuit of a shoe, Josh searches frantically for the phone.

18

"What up, Dad?"

"Son?" Before Tyrone could respond to his pubescent son, Josh jumps right into a conversation.

"Yo Dad, I shaved this morning!" Laughing in the phone, Tyrone asks "You what? - Wait, you shaved what?" he asks jokingly.

"Man, Dad, I was getting stubbly, and I had to - you know, get it smooth for the ladies."

"I see – smooth." Tyrone grins into the phone.

"Umm hmm, well I just hope you know what you're doing, son, and remember what I showed you." Rolling his eyes in the air, Josh replies.

"Yes dad, I do. I mean, I have a couple little nicks, but nothing serious." Scratching his head at the thought, Tyrone responds,

"Oh, Lord. I don't even want to know son."

Changing the subject, he says, "Ok, well, I just wanted to call and say have a great first day of school and that I love you and I am very proud of you."

"Aight, Pop; thanks, love you, too."

"Hey - son!"

"Yeah Dad?"

"Stop harassing your sister please." With a wide boyish grin, Josh replied,

"Yeah, sure, that will be the day. Bye Dad!"

"Love you son. Call me later." Now, painfully aggravated at the lack of time consciousness her children have displayed, Sherita is yelling from the bottom of the stairs at the top of her lungs.

"I am not going to say this anymore, I am just going to leave – now LET'S GO!" Josh comes billowing down the stairs yelling, "I got front!"

Rolling her eyes in disgust, Alana just shakes her head as she grabs her lunch bag off the counter and makes her way to the garage. A trendy upscale area in the suburbs of Atlanta is where the Colemans' call home. Having lived here for the past 10 years, Sherita and the kids remained in the house after an amicable divorce from Tyrone. That was 6 years ago, and Sherita and Tyrone have a really special relationship now, solely focused on the stability, success and happiness of Alana and Josh. Sherita, an Atlanta native, has lived and worked all over the world, from interning as a Communications Specialist in Europe to Corporate Nonprofit Communications in Virginia. An open-minded liberal mom at

39, she loves her children and wants to see them healthy and happy. Tyrone is a financial analyst and executive vice president for a nationwide telecommunications company. A family man, nothing is more important to him than his kids. A dedicated father, he still looks after Sherita from afar even though they are no longer married. Tyrone is a constant figure in Josh and Alana's life. The Coleman kids are your typical teens. Josh plays junior varsity basketball in high school and Alana is a part of the school's glee club and student actor's guild. They are both honor roll students and understand the importance of balance in life. Sherita and Tyrone share joint custody of the kids and in the past have even maintained family vacations together, however, the kids are older and can make their own decisions.

Chapter 2

A typical Monday morning, the school parking lot is a nightmare. All of the freshman parents are parked along the sides seeing their children off to a big new world called high school. Knowing that this will not only be a life-altering turning point in their child's life, but theirs as well. Sherita is visibly frustrated with the traffic and, as usual, is having conversations with the people in the car in front of her as if they can hear every word she is saying.

"Seriously, lady, parking right there makes sense to you?" she voices to herself. Josh is checking out the sights of the freshman girls standing along the sidewalk while bopping his head to music in his headset, he all of a sudden yells.

"HEY MA – LET ME OUT HERE."

Sherita looks at her son with a cold, hard, annoyed stare trying to understand why he thinks he is using a normal voice.

"Josh, boy if you don't take them doggone headphones out of your ear, I swear they are going to be a permanent accessory!"

"Sorry Ma."

"Now leave that CD player in the car please."

"Aww Ma, I was going to listen to it in gym".

"Not today, leave it! Get out my car. Alana! You too, out!"

"Oh my God Ma, are you serious? Please it's just a few more minutes and we will be right there."

"Well, let's just say you will be there sooner, now get out!"

Josh exited the car willingly, as he has spotted a couple of friends over on the side and is happy with the command. Alana, on the other hand, is clearly displeased with having to walk alone like a new student on the first day in a new school. She throws on some dark shades.

"Hey," Sherita yells out the window at the two of them, "make it a great day kids – I will be here when school gets out."

Swirling her finger in the air as if to sarcastically say "woo-hoo," Alana gives a fake smile to her mother and walks away.

With a huge sigh of relief, Sherita says to herself "*Lord, my kids*".

Determined to be on time for her morning appointment, she proceeds to make an illegal u-turn in the parking lot of the prestigious College Hill High School. The school has a majority white population and 4-percent minority representation and is one of the best in the city. They have an outstanding curriculum for students from freshman through senior year and more than 92-percent of their graduates attend Ivy League Colleges and garner full-ride scholarships. Of course, the black students who attend this school are considered snobby, bourgie, want-to-be white kids by students who attend schools in more urban areas.

The final bell rings and students are scattering to make it to homeroom on time. The classroom is loud and unruly. Kids are paired off into groups of two and three discussing summer vacations and nervous jitters about the new school year. Alana sits in front of the room chatting with her friend Janet.

"Hey Lan, what lunch period do you have A or B?"

"Not sure, they messed up my schedule and I think it will be different tomorrow when they put me in the correct class. Right now I have B lunch, which sucks because I have to wait until the end of the day to eat!"

Janet nods with excitement.

"I have B lunch. What class are they changing?"

"They have me in some Early Development class that makes no sense and has nothing to do with anything. So I told them I want to get out of it and hopefully replace it with the advanced health class and get it out the way," Alana replied. "Oh, yeah, I've never heard of "Early Development

Class," Janet replied.

"Right," says Alana with a roll of the eyes.

The girls are distracted by a moderately stern voice in the room.

"All right, all right class lets settle down!"

Their teacher Mrs. Peaty, a 55-year-old, middle-class white lady with

glasses enters the room holding a Dunkin Donuts coffee cup in one hand,

her attendance book in the other. She places her things on the edge of

the wooden desk and turns to locate a piece of chalk to write with. She is

wearing a blue flower print dress with ruffles, panty hose and low-heel

shoes. She starts to speak. Trying to encourage the background chatter in

the room to end, she makes her request one more time.

"Class, settle down. Now, we don't have much time, so when I call your

name please say present and come up and get your locker assignments.

This will also be my mechanism for taking roll today, so if you do not

come to get a locker key, you will be marked absent. So, please pay

attention – I wish to only have to do this once."

Janet leans over and whispers to Alana.

"I hope your locker is next to mine."

Mrs. Peaty starts calling out names as if she is calling out the winning team on a soccer field.

"Janet Brown, please come to the front; Alana Coleman please come to the front; Eric Davis, please…

All of a sudden her flow stops and she is disrupted by a loud clamoring noise. Eric Davis, a known class clown has managed to drop all of his things to the floor. "Sorry," Eric says.

"I didn't realize you were going to call my name so quickly," he said.

Students in the back of the class are snickering and calling Eric names as he makes his way to the front of the class.

"Alright folks, settle down," demanded Mrs. Peaty.

She continued with the locker distributions. Alana and Janet continued to chat quietly focusing on the day ahead and what the other classes and teachers had in store. The bell rang and students dispersed immediately. Disappearing into the hallway, Alana proceeded to look for her locker. With less than 4 minutes until the first class, she had to hurry.

Chapter 3

The Isley Brothers' song "Smooth Sailing" is playing on the radio and

Sherita is stuck in traffic on the way to work singing along to the words.

"Nothing but smooth sailing tonight...."

Looking at the clock, she realizes she is going to be late for her first

meeting. "Dammit!" she exclaims. Going the equivalent of 10 miles-per-

hour north on Interstate 75/85, she is still at least another 20 minutes

away from the office.

"Oh well," she sighs, "guess I will get there when I get there."

Continuing to enjoy the amusement from the morning radio show, as she

passes Turner Field, she sees a welcomed break in the flow of traffic up

ahead.

"Finally, thank you Jesus," she says as traffic abruptly picks up to normal

speed. As she puts the pedal to the metal, Sherita heads for the exit just

off of West Peachtree Street. Turning into the parking deck, she has five

minutes before her meeting with a representative of a local nonprofit

organization. Coming off the elevator, Sherita catches a glimpse of a

tall, dark and extremely handsome man. With no time to waste, she

heads to her office.

"Alicia, has my 9:30 arrived?" She asks her assistant.

"Yes ma'am, he's here should I give you a few minutes?"

"*He?*"

"Yes – *he* is here." Alicia, reiterated.

"Ok, let him know I will be right with him and give me five minutes to get my notes in order," she said.

"Yes ma'am."

Sherita turned her computer on and quickly reviewed her notes before the meeting. "*Hmph, you'd think after being here for 4 years now, nothing would surprise me. But, I guess today is the day that all changes,*" she said to herself.

As she did a quick check of her hair and lipstick in the mirror, she could see through the glass doors that Alicia was escorting the intriguingly handsome man from the lobby to her office.

"Oh my God," she thought to herself, is that the "*he*" she was referring to?

"Shit!"

"Ms. Coleman, this is Mr. Lamont Washington from The Youth in Action Organization of Atlanta," Alicia said.

28

Extending her hand to shake his, Sherita invited Mr. Washington into the office. "Thank you, Alicia."

"Mr. Washington, can I get you anything? A bottle of water or some coffee?" she asked.

"No, I am fine, thank you," he replied.

"Please accept my apology for running late, Atlanta traffic is so unpredictable and unfortunately with it being the first day back to school, I had to rally my kids out of the house this morning."

"No problem, I understand. How many kids do you have?"

"Two, a boy, 16, and a girl, 17, and they are truly a handful."

"I bet," he said.

"Do you have kids?" Sherita asks.

"Yes, twin boys 14."

"Wow, so you know what I'm going through? Please, have a seat," she gestured. As they laughed, they realized they might have a little more in common than they thought.

"Yes, yes I do."

After a few seconds of awkward silence, Sherita realized it was time to get down to business.

"So - Mr. Washington."

"Please call me Lamont," he interrupted. Sherita was blushing.

"So, Lamont – what brings you in today?"

"Well, my company The Youth in Action Organization of Atlanta has established this unique concept for students that I believe your company would want to be a part of and become the title sponsor."

"I'm listening," she said as he paused to ensure that she was following along so far. The room had suddenly gotten a bit warm. Sherita was glad she decided to wear the classic black skirt and white shirt with a fabulous pair of sexy sandals today so she wouldn't look like she was sweating bullets at the moment.

This brother is fine, she thought. Probably 6-foot-3 in height with a strong athletic build, cocoa brown skin and can hang a suit with the best of the best. Umph, brown eyes, beautiful teeth.

"Do you have any questions?" "Hello?" Lamont realized it seemed as though Sherita was lost at some point. "Oh!"

"Sorry, I was making some notes in my head, something you said made me think of some interesting collaborations that could come out of this venture if we were to move forward," she said with confidence and slight

confusion.

"Hopefully, he didn't notice me checking him out, she thought. Oh,

God," she thought, I have not heard a word this man has said."

"Mr. Wash, I mean, Lamont, did you bring a proposal with you outlining

the things you mentioned today?"

"Yes, I have that here – it gives an in-depth description of our

organization and the programs we offer to youth and parents within the

metro Atlanta community. It also outlines the full proposal and the

recommended partnership between your organization and mine."

"Great, I will discuss this with my team and see if there is a way for us to

get involved. While I can't make any promises, I can, however, assure

you that it will be reviewed and given the highest level of consideration."

"We would appreciate that," he said.

"It typically takes 30 days for us to reply. If we are interested in moving

forward, someone from the development team will give you a call with

next-step instructions on your end. If your proposal is not selected or

approved, you will receive a letter and will have to reapply in one year."

"Do you have any additional questions for me?"

"No."

As they both stand at the same time, Sherita extends her hand to shake his again. "Thank you Lamont for coming in, and again I apologize for being late." Enclosing her hand inside of his, he looks her straight in the eyes.

"No problem, it was my pleasure."

Smiling, Sherita responds.

"I will walk you out." *Not a bad start to the day*, she thought.

Sherita proceeded with her morning routine of checking emails and voicemail messages from Friday afternoon. She glanced at her calendar and was pleasantly surprised that she only had one additional meeting scheduled after lunch. This would give her an opportunity to make a few follow-up phone calls.

Chapter 4

Not too bad for a Monday, Sherita thought as she finished checking the last round of emails before she headed out to pick up the kids. It is tradition that Sherita pick up Josh and Alana on the first day since they started school. She always felt it gave her a good sense of how the year would be if she immediately heard the pros and cons from the first day to see what to expect. While the kids never seem to realize what she was doing, they always got in the car with loads of stories to tell. As she headed to her car in the parking lot, she could hear her cellphone ringing in the bottom of her purse. Searching frantically for the chiming Beethoven classic, she managed to locate it just in time.

"Sherita Coleman, how may I help you?" she answered professionally.

"Ms. Coleman?" The deep baritone voice spoke on the other end.

"Yes, this is she."

"This is Lamont Washington."

Standing in the middle of the parking lot, Sherita all of a sudden forgot where she was and exactly what she was doing. As fate would have it, she just couldn't seem to get Mr. Washington off her mind from earlier today. There was something really interesting about him; besides the fact that he was fine as hell.

"Hello." he said.

"Ah...yes, Mr. Washington, I mean – Lamont, is everything OK?"

"Yes, everything is fine. I hope you don't mind, I took the liberty of calling your cellphone from the number on your business card."

"No, no, not at all, how can I help you?" She asked with curiosity as she continued walking.

Finally reaching her car, she gets in and takes a look at her watch as she exits the garage onto Ellis Street.

"I wanted to give you a call and tell you again how appreciative I am for the opportunity to meet with you today. I also wanted to extend an invitation for dinner tonight, if you're available," he asked.

"Dinner?" Sherita asked with intrigue.

"I would like that, however, I am headed to pick up my kids from school. What time and where were you thinking?"

"How does 7:30 sound at Houston's by Lenox?"

"I can probably make that work, thank you – I guess I will see you then?" She said with a smile.

"Perfect, see you then," he said.

As Sherita hung up the phone, she wasn't sure what just happened. It's been at least a year since she had been on a real date and she really just wasn't up for anyone playing games. Although slightly excited, she realized she only had another five or 10 minutes or so before she reached the kids' school. She decided to give her best friend Kendra a real quick call and tell her what had just happened. "Tell me you won the lottery and to meet you at the airport in an hour to head to Jamaica," Kendra blurted out as she answered the phone.

Laughing out loud, Sherita says, "girl, please – I wish, but no; one better."

"What the hell could be better than you winning the lottery?" Kendra asked sarcastically.

"Girl, I got a date!"

"What?!" Kendra was in shock. Since the divorce, Sherita has been very selective about the company she keeps. She is a gorgeous, high profile individual and she can't be seen with just any ol' Pookie or Ray Ray.

"With who, how'd this happen," Kendra inquired.

"I had a meeting with this really nice and REALLY good-looking guy earlier today, and Kendra, there was just something about him. Although I thought no more of it after he left, apparently he did and he called me on my cellphone to ask me out for dinner – TONIGHT!"

"Wow, that is interesting, so – are you going to go?"

"Duh, yeah….we are meeting tonight at 7:30 at Houston's around Lenox." "Hmm.." Kendra said.

"Why Houston's?"

"Hell, I don't know, I was just in shock of the fact that the brother called my cellphone and asked me out…why? What's wrong with Houston's?"

"Nothing, just an interesting choice. Well, I guess you got a date Ms. Coleman!" "Yeah, I guess so – OK look, so I am pulling up at the school to get the kids, I will call you after I leave the restaurant and tell you what I think," Sherita said.

"You better – because I hate to have to show up at Houston's and sit in the booth behind you guys shooting croutons from my salad across the room," Kendra said. "Bye girl – call you later; love you."

"Love you, too – hey; be careful."

"I will."

As Sherita hung up the phone, she could see her kids standing a few feet away from one another waiting for her to arrive. When she pulled up, the usual mad dash for the front seat ensued with Alana winning the battle this time.

"Yo, Ma – what up?" chimes Josh as he slides in the car.

"Hey son – how was school?"

"Hello mother," says Alana in a voice that gives the indication that her story is sure to be full of drama."

"Hey guys, how was your first day?" she asks.

"It was no big deal, my locker doesn't work and it is on the bottom," Josh says. "Well, my day was just GRAND, mother," Alana says sarcastically.

"Grand – huh, she says with a mocking tone. What made it 'just' grand Alana? "Mom, they completely screwed up my schedule. I am seriously trying to get all the major classes out of the way early so the last part of the year I can just breeze through, but NOOO they put me into some stupid Early Development class! I already can't wait for this year to be over," Alana sighs.

"Oh honey, I'm sorry. Maybe you should see if you could get it switched tomorrow."

"Hey Mom, can we stop by the mall? I need to pick up some jeans for the party after the game next Friday," Josh blurts out.

"What party? And who says you're going to be there? No, we don't have time to stop at the mall," Sherita chimes.

"Mom, why not? We have to drive right past it and it will only take a second." "Listen, I have to drop the two of you off at the house, and run out for a dinner meeting."

Sherita hadn't been on a real date in a year and she and her ex Tyrone had agreed early on that they wouldn't bring multiple people in and out of the kids' lives. She was a bit hesitant to reveal to them that she had been asked out by a guy. Perhaps she was being a little too optimistic in considering it a date.

"Oh Mom, are you serious?" Alana cried out as if she were in agonizing pain.

"I shouldn't be too long, honey, but I will need you to fix dinner for you and Josh." Completely not in agreement with this plan of action, Josh blurts out,

"Gross, just kill me now mom!"

"Shut-up, Josh!" Alana said.

Rolling her eyes, Sherita quickly realizes this date may be just what she needs in her life. As they pull in the driveway, Sherita is all of a sudden consumed with what to wear. Should she change clothes or should she not look to obvious and just keep on her work clothes? After all, he really didn't give her much notice, so perhaps just a quick freshen up of the hair and a spray of perfume should do it. She looked really cute in her black skirt, white silk top, and high-heeled sandals. Cute was never her problem; she always managed to look good even when she wasn't trying.

When they enter the house, the phone is ringing off the hook. They didn't make it in time to answer and neither of them seemed swayed at the idea; it wasn't unusual for them to let the answering machine screen most calls. As everyone dispersed throughout the house in their usual manner, Sherita proceeded to her room to make sure she was still intact. With the way Atlanta traffic is during the week, it had taken them what seemed like hours to get home. Looking at the clock it was now 6:45 p.m. and Sherita realized if she was going to make it there on time, she needed to be leaving the house in the next few minutes. As she hurries through the house, she grabs her purse and calls out, "kids"? Hearing the thumping sounds from the song "I Like," by Guy blaring from Josh's room, she realized it made no sense to attempt to reach him. She quickly pokes her head into Alana's room, who is lying across the bed as if she is trying to take a nap.

"Alana, honey Mommy is leaving, please remember to fix something for you and your brother to eat for dinner. You may even be able to get away with hotdogs and fries," she says.

"Ummhmm," Alana responds.

"I shouldn't be too long, I will call when I am headed back home."

"Have fun, Mother," says Alana as she reaches for the phone to call Janet.

"That is the plan, sweetie! That is the plan," Sherita chimed.

Chapter 5

Looking at her watch, Sherita realized she actually made it to
Buckhead in really good time. It's just 7:20 and Lamont should be
arriving shortly. While she waits, she decides to hit Kendra up real
quick. Kendra and Sherita have been friends since middle school and
have literally been inseparable since the first day they met on the bus ride
home. Kendra is really a sister to Sherita and she couldn't imagine her
life without her in it. Kendra's no-nonsense personality is a welcome
balance to Sherita's laid back easy-go-lucky demeanor. There wasn't
much the two of them didn't share with each other. They have always
vowed to be best friends forever. As the phone rang continuously for
what seemed like an eternity, Sherita noticed Lamont pulling up to the
valet in a nice black Mercedes Benz. She quickly hung up the phone, but
realized she didn't want to seem as though she had been waiting
anxiously, so she pretended to be on the phone as he walked in the door.

"OK, thank you for your call," she pretended – "I will be in touch with
you tomorrow."

Snapping closed her flip phone; Sherita ended her pretend call and stood
to greet Lamont with a handshake.

"Sorry about that," she said. "Just finishing up some work from earlier today."

Flashing a million-dollar smile, Lamont replies, "I understand."

Dismissing her handshake, he instead leaned in for a hug.

"Hello, how are you all?" the hostess asked.

"Dinner for two?"

"Yes," Lamont answered.

"Ok, right this way."

Lamont steps to the side and allows Sherita the right of way. He was excited to get to know her outside of work. As they followed the young lady, she seated them in a booth area near the window. The perfect gentleman, Lamont waited until Sherita took her seat before he took his.

"So, Ms. Coleman," he said slyly.

"Ahhhh, that would be Sherita," she said as she playfully cleared her throat.

"Ok, Sherita – how was the rest of your day?"

"It was a pretty good day," she says, "no complaints. The busiest part of the day was picking up my kids from school."

"Ahh, yeah, first day right?"

"Yes, first day, and it has become tradition, that I always pick them up on the first day to get the first-hand update of how the day went."

"Wow, that's impressive," he says.

"Yeah, I suppose," she replied.

"How about your kids? Are they in school here in Atlanta?" she asked.

"Yes, they live up in Cobb County and attend school out there. They live with their mother," he replied.

"I see. Well, with that, how was your day, and tell me, what landed me this opportunity to do dinner with you?"

Flashing that million-dollar smile again, Lamont replied, "my day was very good, thank you."

"However, I must admit – when I saw you this morning I was mesmerized by your beauty."

"Is that a line Mr. Washington?" she asks with a playful smile.

With a light chuckle, he looks at her and says, "no – not at all. It is the truth. Honestly, I went back and forth in my head for about an hour as to whether or not I would even call and ask you out. I was almost hoping to get your voicemail, to avoid you saying no."

Blushing and smiling quite obviously Sherita says, "I don't believe that for one minute."

"It is true. There was something about you when you got off the elevator and when I realized it was you I would be meeting with, I got extremely nervous." The waitress brings over a bottle of Chardonnay and asks if they are ready to order. They both make a seafood selection from the menu and proceed with the inquisitory conversation.

"Hmm, I must admit, there was something interesting about you as well," Sherita replied. "At first, I thought we had met somewhere before."

"Well, today was obviously meant to happen," Lamont said.

"I guess so," Sherita said. As the two lifted their glasses in a toast to what appeared to be an act of fate, they continued to engross themselves in meaningful conversation that would continue until close to 11:00 p.m. Realizing they were the last couple in the restaurant, Sherita says jokingly, "Well, Mr. Washington, I mean, Lamont – it looks like the restaurant is doing everything short of turning off the lights to get us to leave."

"I see," he replied, "I guess that means you will have to agree to go out with me again in order for us to finish this discussion."

"Well, I guess I will," she says.

As they waited out front for the valet, the two ran down their schedules over the next few days to see where there may be an opportunity for another dinner. Coming up with a Saturday afternoon brunch, the two called it a date. Lamont agreed to connect with Sherita in the next few days to confirm the date, time and location. As he walks her to her car, he plants a nice kiss on the side of her forehead. She thanks him for a great dinner and conversation.

"I will give you a call in a few days," Lamont said again.

"Great."

Driving in silence for a few minutes, Sherita was basking in the moment. She finally turns on the radio and dreams away to the smooth sounds of Barry White's "Secret Garden".

The conversation at dinner with Lamont was nice. It had been a long time since Sherita had this type of giddy feeling for anyone. As she pulls into the garage, Sherita notices every light in the house is on, which means her children are still up and stirring about. Entering the house, see sees the TV is blaring in the front room and Alana is on the sofa on the phone and Josh is in his room playing video games. "Hey Mom, how was dinner?" Alana asks.

"Dinner was good, but you need to get off the phone young lady – it is after 11 o'clock and tomorrow is a school day."

"Josh," she yells as she heads down the hall toward his room.

Entering her son's room, she sees him sitting on the floor in front of the TV playing Super Mario Brothers. He briefly looks up from the game and acknowledges her presence.

"What up, Ma?"

"Hey son, let's get ready for tomorrow, it is a school night."

Finally headed to her room to settle down for the night, Sherita hears her phone ringing.

"Girl, why haven't you called me?" Kendra insisted.

"I have been waiting to hear about this hot date. So, how did it go?"

Kendra's constant support of her friend was always a comforting thing for Sherita. She and Kendra could spend hours at a time on the phone as if they were back in high school. As Sherita settled in for the night and managed to get the kids ready for the next day, she took great pleasure in spending the next hour and a half telling her best friend about the most amazing evening she had had in a long time. One day at a time is all she could think about, but it was a nice feeling.

"Sherita's got a boyfriend. Sherita's got a boyfriend," Kendra playfully sang in the phone before hanging up.

"Bye, Silly," she replied blushing.

Chapter 6

The week seemed to be rounding out pretty nicely. Sherita was looking forward to sleeping in and doing a little shopping Saturday. The kids typically went with their dad on the weekends or really whenever they wanted. This weekend, their dad was hosting an end of summer bar-be-que and wanted the kids to come over. Tyrone was planning on making a huge announcement and wanted the kids to be there to celebrate.

As Sherita finished preparing for work, she noticed that the message indicator light was blinking on the cordless phone. Searching the closet for a pair of blue pumps, she listened intently to the message. Suddenly distracted, she stood speechless for what seemed like forever. The message was from her old friend Allison indicating that she really needed to speak with Sherita and could she contact her as soon as possible. Allison and Sherita were really good friends at one point in life, but then, one day out of the blue, Allison just stopped calling and stopped accepting calls from Sherita. Disturbed by this sudden end to a 10-year long friendship, Sherita beat herself up for years trying to understand what had gone wrong and what she had done that would cause such an abrupt end.

Over the years, Sherita tossed about several scenarios that would help her feel better about the split, but eventually she just had to force herself to realize that whatever had happened, it was apparently something that Allison needed to deal with. She missed their friendship and couldn't help fighting back tears as she listened to the message. Snapping back to reality, Sherita had a wave of emotions flowing through her all at the same time. She was initially angry at the fact that Allison would all of a sudden call her after five years of no contact. But she was extremely concerned just hearing the fragileness in Allison's voice, she felt like she really needed to be there for her friend. But then again, why should she care? As she stood there in a daydream, her thoughts were interrupted by the voice of Alana.

"Mom....Mom!" "Is everything alright?"

"Huh? Oh, yes sweetie, I'm sorry, I just had something on my mind."

"Are you sure?" Alana asks with a look of concern on her face.

"Yeah, yeah...I'm good. You guys ready to go?" Sherita asked as she changed the subject.

"Yep," replied Alana. " I just need to grab my sweater."

As Alana headed down the hall she yells to tell her brother to wrap it up.

49

"Josh! Mom is ready to go!"

Sherita was unusually silent on the ride to school. Her mind was racing a mile a minute flip-flopping back and forth between the voicemail from Allison, to the thought of why she hadn't heard from Lamont since their date Monday night. Surprisingly, she enjoyed his company, conversation and could explore learning more about him. But, right now, she needed to focus on the fact that it is Friday and the kids are about to get out of the car for school and she won't see them again until next week sometime.

"Ok, guys don't forget your Dad is picking you up from school today. Hopefully you brought everything you need to take to his house this weekend, because I am sure he will not be happy about having to back track to pick up anything."

"Got it, hey Mom, let me out here," Josh insisted, half-listening to a word Sherita was saying.

"Ok Mom – don't miss us too much," Alana says.

"Oh, ok...I will try to come to grips with my loneliness," Sherita said jokingly.

As they each chuckled at their sarcastic banter, the kids both reached over and kissed their mother on the cheek.

"Love you, guys," she said.

"Love you, too," they both chime back in unison.

"Ok, now – let's settle in for the traffic," she sighs to herself as she pulls away. Once Sherita got on the highway she decided to give Kendra a call to tell her about the message from Allison. Not always a fan of Allison's, Kendra would at least provide honest feedback as to whether or not Sherita should return the call. Kendra always felt like Allison was too needy of a person and wasn't the type of friend to Sherita that Sherita had always been to her. Sherita was always open-minded and loved both of them as individuals and felt like Kendra was being too hard on Allison at times. Kendra answered the phone on the first ring saying… "Ok, what now, you and lover boy going to make it official?"

"Huh," Sherita says laughing in the phone. "Girl, are you crazy? What are you talking about?"

Kendra, laughing pretty hard at this point says, "Sherita, you never call me this early in the morning unless it is something pretty important, so I figured it must have something to do with Mr. Tall, Dark and Handsome."

"Girl, I wish," says Sherita, "honestly I haven't heard from him in a couple of days, I may try to give him a call later this afternoon, but, no, that is not why I am calling."

A little concerned at this revelation, Kendra says "really, how long is a couple of days?"

"Huh?" asks Sherita. Not really sure why this is the conversation they are having. "What kind of question is that, a couple of days, two."

"Hmm," Kendra replies, "you don't think he's married do you?"

"What!? Married. Girl, no – he is not married and that is not why I am calling you this morning."

However, the thought had crossed Sherita's mind. What if Lamont really was married and was trying to run game? Sherita rolled her eyes at the thought. "Anyway," she says, somewhat aggravated – "I am calling because I checked my messages at the house this morning and I had this voicemail from Allison."

"Allison who?" Kendra said sarcastically.

"Allison, Allison," Sherita says, "what do you mean Allison who?"

"Umph, what the hell does she want?" Kendra asked displeasingly.

"Hell, I don't know, I haven't called her back, but Kendra she sounded like something is really wrong, what do you think?"

"Hmph…seriously, you're asking me? You know how I feel about that whole situation with her, but knowing you, you're going to call anyway."

"Are you saying I shouldn't?"

"Hell yeah! That crazy-ass girl hasn't called in what, four or five years and now all of a sudden out the blue she leaves a message on your phone sounding in distress, how the hell did she get your number anyway? I say don't call back, shit, if it is that important she'll call again."

At this point, Sherita was confused. Perhaps Kendra was right. It had been quite a while since Sherita had actually spoken to Allison and she had never returned any of Sherita's calls over the years. Maybe she should wait to see if Allison calls again and not rush to conclusions like she always had in the past where Allison was concerned.

"Ok, Kendra you're right."

"Hell, I know I am right – that's why you called me," Kendra continued.

"I'll just wait and see if she reaches out again, and go from there.

Hopefully everything is alright with her and it isn't something serious.

Well, I am pulling into my parking garage."

Sherita lied she was still at least five minutes away. She needed a minute

to process everything and see how to proceed.

"I don't want the call to drop when I turn in, I will give you a call later

this afternoon."

"Ok," said, Kendra. "Have a good day."

"I will," Sherita replied, "you, too."

"Hey," Kendra blurted out before Sherita could hang up the phone.

"Yeah?" "Don't worry about it, if it is important, she will call back."

"I know, love you girl."

"Love you, too."

Chapter 7

Running down the hall, Josh is frantically trying to get to class before the bell rings. Making it in the nick of time, he hears the blaring sound from the loud speaker just as he plops down into his seat. With a room full of chatter going on all around him, he quickly gives a what-up nod to his boys Aaron and Demetri. The three of them have been friends since elementary school and live on the same street.

"Man, Josh, where were you, dog? You almost didn't make it," Demetri asks. With a long sigh, out of breath and shaking his head, Josh replies, man I had to walk Tracy to class. You know I am thinking about asking her to the dance Friday night after the game."

"Tracy?" Aaron says in shock, "man you are way out of your league dude; she is way too fine for your crazy ass."

Laughing at his friend's keen sense of humor, Josh just looks at them both and says, "yeah alright, then why did she give me her phone number?"

"What!" the boys said at once. "She must be hallucinating," Aaron chimed. "Yeah, man she's feelin' me, don't hate cause a brotha got mad moves," Josh said jokingly.

"Yo, I thought we were all going to the game and the dance together," said Demetri with a hint of dismay.

"Yeah, that was what we discussed way before school started back," co-signed Aaron, "now you gone change the plans for some girl? Dude you trippin'!"

"Fellas, fellas, we can all still go to the game and the dance together, all you two hard legs need to do is find two more chicks to go with and we can make it one big happy family event. See, problem solved!" Josh boasted with a grin on his face. Not all together happy with their friend's sudden change of plans, both Demetri and Aaron kind of liked the idea of having dates themselves, except, who would they ask?

As the class is brought under attention by Mr. Harrison the history teacher, he directs the students to open their textbooks to chapter three. "For those of you who were paying attention earlier this week, please pass your take-home assignments up to the front. For those of you who turn in this assignment today, I will give an extra credit grade of 100 points to be utilized later in the year. These additional points may be of great benefit to your grades. For those of you who chose not to comply with this week's assignment, you have until Monday to turn it in and you will suffer a 10-point deduction for turning it in late. As the room erupted in what seemed like a well-choreographed teeth-sucking musical, many of the students gave verbal indication of their lack of responsibility pertaining to their homework. Josh, on the other-hand was the only one who had his to turn in, although he acts like the class clown most of the time, he takes his schoolwork very seriously. His parents don't accept excuses when it comes to maintaining an A and B average, and both Josh and Alana make sure they are on point. Josh has been a pretty popular young man ever since elementary school. Even as an 11th grader, he was already pushing 6 feet tall, smooth chocolate-colored brown skin, with disgustingly perfectly straight white teeth, big brown eyes and long eyelashes. An avid sports enthusiast, his passion was basketball. Having played since Little League, he pretty much walked on to the Junior Varsity squad once he made it to high school. Josh had a plan for his future. And he wanted to ensure that he did his part in high school to accomplish those goals. Playing college ball was the ultimate goal.

"Dude, you actually did your homework?" quizzed Demetri.

"Yeah, man. When did you have time to do all of that?" inquired Aaron.

"Yo, I do my homework every night, man, I don't have time to be messing around with you guys. I suggest you all get it together now. Man we are only a few years away from graduation and scholarships are plenty," Josh chimed.

"All right class, let's get started. I suggest you all take note of this week's homework assignment on the board and prepare to meet the deadline," mentioned Mr. Harrison. As Josh focused on today's assignment, he couldn't help but think about Tracy. Although he felt good about getting her number earlier, he wasn't quite sure if she liked him enough to go to the dance with him this week after the game. Josh had a plan and it would start with attempting to walk Tracy to class every day this week and carrying her books. After all, he was a smooth operator. Hopefully, that would be the icing on the cake to get her to say yes. Now, he just needed to help his buddies find a date and his plan would work brilliantly.

Chapter 8

As the bell rings, Alana and Janet make their way to lunch. While they are walking and chatting with one another someone comes up behind them and taps Alana on the shoulder. When she turns around, she is mesmerized by the image that stands before her.

"Hi Alana," says the young man. "How are you?"

Standing with her mouth wide open enough to hold a beehive inside, Alana was in shock at who she was seeing before her, as she composed herself she says, "Delton? Delton Jemison?"

"In the flesh," said Delton, as he flashed this Ronnie DeVoe from New Edition smile and rocked this L.L. Cool J muscle-bound body.

"Oh, my God, what are you doing here?" she asked in amazement.

"I thought you moved away. What happened?"

As Alana continued with her mini-interrogation of the seemingly "not-so-new" kid, Janet intentionally cleared her throat in an attempt to get her friend to make some introductions.

"Oh, my bad. Delton Jemison, this is my best friend Janet Brown." The two shook hands and there was an instant interest on the part of Janet. However, Delton had something else in mind.

"Wow, I can't believe it's you," Alana said. "You're all grown up now."

Blushing slightly, Delton replied, "yep it's me. You guys mind if I join you for lunch?"

Janet quickly replies, "nope, we don't mind at all!"

As Alana and Delton continued their conversation down memory lane, he shared that he and his family moved back to Atlanta from Florida over the summer. His parents had recently gotten divorced and his mom wanted to come back to Atlanta. Delton and Alana were neighbors in the old neighborhood. Having attended Montessori school together up until third grade, the two were always like peas in a pod. Alana knew something was going on with the Jemison family, but back then, as a kid, it wasn't your place to be in grown-folks business. She remembers being sad when they moved away and wondering if she would ever see her friend again. Little did she know, the answer to that question would be yes and he would grow up to be such a cutie-pie.

As the trio made their way through the line, it appeared as though there were others in the room who had noticed the good-looking new kid on the block. Girls of all shapes and sizes made their way past the group's table and all of a sudden had something to say. One girl even went so far as to come over and ask to borrow a pencil just to look Delton in the eyes. With only a few minutes left until the bell rang, Delton asked Alana for her number and wanted to know if he could come by this weekend to see her brother and her parents. Alana complied on the part of the phone number, but revealed to Delton, that her parents had also gone through a divorce and life in the Coleman household was quite different than what he remembered growing up. Janet insisted she and Delton exchange numbers as well, and asked if Delton had any plans to attend the first football game of the year. Delton agreed to join the girls for the game and dance Friday night he was excited to rekindle his relationship with Alana.

The first warning bell sounded and the three had to immediately break up their reunion. Headed to class, Janet decided to run to the locker she and Alana shared. Alana and Delton headed up the hall. Realizing they were still talking, they both ultimately ended up in the same place, Ms. Stewart's drama class. "Wow, is this your class?" Alana asked.

"Yep, looks like it," he replied.

"Cool, you will love Ms. Stewart, she is a great teacher and she makes this class fun. She has been my drama teacher since my freshman year," Alana said.

Delton opened the door for Alana and with a pleased look on his face he thought to himself, that he already loved the class. Because it was a drama class, the group did not operate in a traditional-class manner. The desks were all arranged in a large circle where the students faced each other. Making room for a seat next to her, Alana invited Delton to sit and introduced him to a few students who were sitting to both their left and their right.

"Hello everyone," said a soft voice.

Ms. Stewart is a petite woman in her early 30s who did a tremendous amount of arts and entertainment on Broadway and across the world. Alana was in awe of Ms. Stewart. She started out as a young actress out of Detroit who followed her dreams of moving to New York to star on Broadway. After realizing her dream, she wanted to make an even greater difference in her craft and decided to move to Atlanta to teach drama to aspiring high school students. She still performed in local theater and plays from time-to-time.

"Class, it looks like we have a new student with us today, let's give him a few minutes to introduce himself."

With all eyes on the new kid, the whispers in the room have created a light crowd of chatter. Clearing his throat, Delton commands the attention of the room.

"Um, hey everybody, my name is Delton Jemison, I just moved back to Atlanta from Miami, Florida, where I have lived for the past seven years. I have been taking acting classes for the past five years and have been fortunate enough to have done a few national commercials with JC Penney and Sears, as well as performed in local dinner theaters down in Florida. Um, I am also a football player and I enjoy hanging out and that's all I can think of," he said. Learning more and more by the minute, Alana had no idea that Delton had blossomed into such an all-around talented guy and handsome, too. Sitting down, he whispered in her ear, "whew, glad that's over."

"Ok, class today is the day that we will start working on creating and developing our own version of the classic love story Romeo and Juliet. As you know, this play was written by William Shakespeare. It is the tale of two young lovers whose deaths ultimately unite their feuding families. It is by far, Shakespeare's most popular play about teenage love and has been re-enacted on stages across the country for decades. Everyone will have an opportunity to audition for the characters in the play, however, the important thing to remember is that I am looking for talent that can maintain the energy of the original production, while adding a creative, ethnic spin on the story that will keep the audience in awe. We will perform this classic in the spring. So while we have some time to opening night, there is still a lot to be done in the process from casting, to set building, to production, stage management and promotions. There will be something for everyone to do. Please keep in mind that this play will count as your final exam. So, whatever your role ends up being, you will be graded accordingly based upon how intently you perform and carry out your duties and responsibilities. Each class will be dedicated to learning about the history of the arts and we will do some skit reviews, however, you all will be expected to work on the project in your own time in an effort to maintain your grades. There will be periodic tests and quizzes that may pertain directly to the material and other information that will be discussed in class. I encourage each of you to take good notes because they will help you in the end. The lead characters will be selected the first week in January. So - any questions?" As the group looked around the room at one another and no one wanting to be the first person to raise their hands, there was a silent agreement that each person would wait until the next class to figure out what they wanted to tackle in this project.

"Well, if there are no questions, let me hand out a script to each of you to start studying. Do not lose these scripts, as you will not be receiving another copy. I expect that you will have them with you for every class and/or meeting and that you will take care of them. While I am passing out the scripts, there is a sign-in sheet going around the room. Please put your name on the sheet and indicate your initial area of interest for the play. This sheet will also serve as my role-call mechanism for today so I encourage everyone to fill it out for credit for today's class."

After Ms. Stewart finished handing out the scripts to the class, she discussed the basics of acting and the importance of teamwork. The bell rang and the group scattered and they headed toward the last class of the day.

"Delton, it is good seeing you, please feel free to call me this weekend and we will catch up. I will be at my Dad's house, but we should be able to chat," Alana said. "I most certainly will," Delton replied.

"Ok, well, I need to stop by my locker before my last class and get my stuff, so I will holla at you later," she said.

"Ok, thanks again Alana, it was good running into you."

Feeling good about this reunion with Alana, he knew that this was going to be a great senior year. He was also pleasantly surprised to see that they both would be auditioning for the lead roles in the Romeo and Juliet play, which would give him more time to spend with Alana and hopefully win her heart.

Chapter 9

Sherita opened her eyes to the sound of a loud blaring noise. A bit confused and delusional, she reached over to hit the snooze button, but realized that it wasn't the alarm clock, it was her ringing cellphone.

"Hello," she says in a whisper and glancing at the clock.

Trying to understand if her eyes were deceiving her, she saw that it appeared to be 5:45 a.m. Thinking to herself something must be wrong, because who would be calling me at this ungodly hour on a Saturday morning.

"Hi beautiful," said the deep voice on the other end of the phone.

"Um, hello," Sherita said again even more discombobulated.

"Hey you, I know it's early, but I wanted to hear your voice," he said.

"Lamont," Sherita asked in shock. She hadn't heard from Lamont since they had dinner a few weeks ago and she had pretty much chalked it up to him not being as interested in her as she thought he was.

"Um, hey, how are you? Is everything OK, why are you calling so early?"

"Yeah, yeah, baby – everything is good. I know it's been a minute since you and I spoke and I apologize for that, I have had some family issues

67

going on and just been running trying to get stuff handled. I know it is early, but I wanted to see if you would meet me for breakfast this morning so that I can make up for my sudden disconnectivity over the past few days?"

"Breakfast," Sherita, said sternly, as she looked at the clock again. She had to make sure she wasn't dreaming.

"Lamont, it is 5:45 in the morning and you are calling me asking me to go to breakfast? Are you serious?"

"Sherita, I know, I am sorry for calling so early, sweetheart, but like I said I want to see you and I want to talk to you and explain my absence, so please, will you agree to meet me for breakfast?"

Lamont pleaded with Sherita. He knew he was taking a risk by making this call, but there was something about her that he just could not shake. He had thought about her intently since that night at dinner and really was working on getting some things straight in his life before he pursued this friendship with Sherita. His track record with women had always ended with a trail of drama in his past. Lamont was determined to turn over a new leaf in life and he felt like he could start over with Sherita.

"Listen, I know you're upset and you have every right to be, but the bottom line of it is that I can't stop thinking about you and I just want to see you. So, if you would, please meet me at 9:00 a.m. There is a really nice little breakfast spot down in Virginia Highland that serves the best vegetable omelets and banana nut pancakes. PLEEEZZZEE," he said jokingly.

Sherita was a bit intrigued to hear Lamont's story, and even though it was early, she agreed to meet him later that morning at 9:00.

"Yes, Lamont, I will meet you for breakfast. See you there."

Before he had an opportunity to carry on a conversation Sherita immediately hung up the phone without saying goodbye. As her mind began to wonder aimlessly, she laid there for a bit wondering what exactly Lamont meant by him needing to handle some family business? She thought to herself hopefully it isn't anything too serious, because she is certainly not in the mood for drama, especially someone else's.

Taking another look at the clock, it was now 6:20 in the morning. It was too early to give Kendra a call and tell her the latest news on Lamont and besides, she kind of wanted to wait to hear what the brother had to say before she shared the update with her friend. As she continued to run through the thoughts in her head, Sherita felt the best thing she should do was pray. She started talking out loud to God, as she oftentimes did, just seeking his direction and continued guidance. "Lord, I come to you right now to say thank you for your continued guidance and protection over my life," she prayed.

Thinking about all that she had endured in her life, Sherita had lots to be thankful for. She had managed to keep her head above the fray that seemed to follow some of her girlfriends and she didn't take that favor in life for granted. Somewhere in between her thoughts of gratefulness and thoughts of Lamont, she dozed back off to sleep. When she woke up, it was 8:30 and she realized she was running extremely late. Needing to jump in the shower and throw on something quick, she was surely not going to make it to the restaurant until closer to 9:30. Leaving the house at exactly nine o'clock, she headed toward Virginia Highland. Luckily, there wasn't much traffic on the road so she may not be as late as she had anticipated. Sherita decided to call Kendra anyway. As the phone rang two, three and four times, Sherita was in the middle of her voicemail message when Kendra beeped in on the other line.

"Hey girl, you up?" Sherita asked all bubbly.

"I am up, but just laying here, what's up with you? Sounds like you are up and out this morning," Kendra replied.

"Well, let's just say I have been up since about 5:45 this morning," Sherita said. "What!"

"Why in the hell would you be up at 5:45 on a Saturday morning, did something happen?"

Kendra tried to sound supportive, but knew that it was going to be an interesting story from her sister-friend.

"So," Sherita started off.

"Oh Lord," Kendra said.

Sherita and Kendra had been friends long enough to know just by the first words out of their mouths what type of conversations were in store and at the top of the "girl let me tell you this" list was a sentence that started with the word "so". Sucking her teeth, Sherita sighed in the phone and said, "come on Kendra, listen I only have a few minutes to talk."

Thoroughly intrigued at this point, Kendra anxiously agreed and allowed her friend to move forward with her marathon menagerie of a story.

Sherita started off again. "So, I get this phone call at 5:30 this morning

71

and surprisingly enough it was Lamont asking me to meet him this morning for breakfast," Sherita said hurriedly. "Wait, a damn, minute," Kendra said.

"Wait, wait hold on Kendra let me finish," insisted Sherita.

"Ok," Kendra said, "keep going."

With an exhausting sigh, Sherita realized she was right in front of the restaurant and would have to continue this conversation with Kendra later.

"Girl, I am here now, so I will call you as soon as I leave and get back in the car." "So what! He hasn't called in two weeks his ass can wait a few more minutes," Kendra said.

"I know! I know! But I was supposed to be here at 9:00 and I am extremely late. I promise I will call as soon as I get back in the car!"

"Aight," Kendra said and the two hung up.

As Sherita entered the restaurant, she thought either everyone in Virginia Highlands is sleeping in or this restaurant is dead. She saw Lamont sitting at a table in the back near the picture window overlooking a serene view of a flower garden and waterfall pool. As she approached the table, Lamont stood to greet her with a hug and kiss on the cheek.

"Good morning beautiful, I was beginning to think you weren't going to show up," he said coyly.

"Yeah, well, would have served you right had I not," she shot back quickly.

"Ok, Ok, I deserve that," he said with his hands up in the air.

"Ok, well, I am here now and please accept my apology for being late, but I actually overslept after I received this god-awful phone call at 5:30 in the morning. But, hey a girl has to make up her beauty sleep," she said jokingly.

Lovingly smiling at her, Lamont admired her in awe.

"So, why is the restaurant empty?" she finally asked.

"Well, that's what I was hoping to surprise you with, but you were reminiscing about your beauty sleep," he said jokingly.

"Listen, Sherita, I know that I have been somewhat missing in action the past few weeks and I have really been trying to think of how to call you and apologize and ask if I could start over with you. I really like you and believe it or not, I just can't seem to stop thinking about you and I want to get to know you and make you smile. So, I reached out to my man Todd, who owns this place, and asked him if he would help me make this morning special. As it turns out, the restaurant will be closed today anyway as they prepare for a dinner reception later tonight, but he agreed to allow me to shower you with the tantalizing tastes of his Master Chef Rob for a one-on-one breakfast entrée. So, please sit, enjoy the mimosas, the fruit and the music and Chef Rob will prepare a delectable meal that is sure to put a smile on your face."

Surprised and overwhelmed at the same time, Sherita tried her best not to show the level of excitement on her face. However, the blushing got the best of her and she had to reveal that she was impressed by this move and had to give the brotha some cool points.

"Thank you Lamont, I love it," she said as she reached over and touched his hand. "Great," he replied.

"I really want to show you the world, and I want us to start off on the right track." "Look, I have to share with you the reason why I have been out of pocket the past few weeks. I have been handling some unfinished business with my children's mother. She and I have been going through a grueling back-and-forth custody battle and it has truly taken a lot out of me. I am really not one to have or involve myself in drama, but this has been a situation that is beyond my control. She has not gotten past the fact that we are not going to be together, and, as a result, is determined to make my life miserable. Over the past few weeks, we have been finalizing our agreement regarding our kids in court and I just didn't want to subject you to that madness. So I felt it would be best to get that stuff under wraps and then start over with you."

"Look, I understand that you have issues with your ex-wife Lamont, but it was aggravating that you would just not call at all and say anything. Honestly, I just thought you were not interested and not man enough to say that."

"No, no, no, sweetheart, please know that it was nothing like that at all," he said shaking his head. "Listen, like I told you at dinner the first day I met you, I was interested in getting to know you and seeing how you and I could form a friendship and I mean that from the bottom of my heart. Even if we don't develop into anything more, I hope that we can still be cool enough to have dinner or breakfast every now and then. But trust me when I tell you, the mere fact that you are here now, shows me that you are a special woman who is respectable, caring and forgiving and I intend to do all that I can do to move us forward in whatever God has in store for us together."

Sherita could sense the sincerity in Lamont's voice and realized he seemed to be really trying to make it all right in his world. As the conversation continued, Chef Rob and a couple of servers approached the table with what looked like enough food to feed a small army. Overwhelmed by the beautiful display of food, Sherita was ready to eat. As Chef Rob presented his array of passion fruit pancakes, eggs, grits and pan-seared salmon, Lamont blessed the food. After taking a few bites of the scrumptious meal, Sherita took it upon herself to make a statement to Lamont.

"Look," she said, as she dabbed the sides of her mouth with her napkin. "Lamont, I like you and I am also interested in getting to know you better, but let me be extremely clear to you now so that, should we move forward, there won't be any room for uncertainty about what I expect or what you can expect from me. First of all, I am good with me. I am not looking for a man to change my world, my environment or make false promises he has no intentions on keeping. I don't do drama, I don't play games and I expect honesty, respect and communication at all times, because that is exactly what you will get from me. I am sorry you are going through a trying time with your ex, and as I mentioned earlier, I get that. But please know, I don't have those issues and because I don't have those types of issues you will never have to worry about being involved in that level of confusion in my life and, therefore, I will not be a part of it in yours. So, if you think that this drama you are experiencing may take a few more weeks to pan out before you get your life back, then I am going to have to say up front thank you for breakfast and call me back in a few weeks, cause I don't do other people's drama. Now, I hate to sound brash or however you take it, but I just know what I don't wish to subject my life to."

Looking at her with loving eyes, Lamont realized that he was in love. The days would turn into months after that breakfast and Lamont and Sherita quickly became involved on a more intimate level. The two spent most of their free time together. So much so, that Lamont had practically moved in with Sherita and the kids. They seemed to be happy in their new space and life was good until Lamont starting noticing some financial discrepancies in his organization's books. He needed to get to the bottom of it and quick.

Chapter 10

The traffic in the school parking lot was bumper-to-bumper, as Sherita inched her way to a suitable drop off point for the kids. Alana, Janet, Josh and Demetri were carrying on nervous chatter among themselves waiting for instructions as to where they would be picked up. It was the first school dance of the year and the entire school had been all abuzz about who was going to show up with whom and the big game. The football team managed to win earlier that day against longtime rival DuPont High School by a close 20 – 23.

"All right guys, this is as close as I am going to get," Sherita said. "Remember, I will be somewhere in this line at 12 o'clock midnight on the dot, anybody that is not out here when I pull up will be subjected to finding their own way home!"

Sherita always had to give a reminder speech to her children whenever she let them take part in extracurricular activities. Both Josh and Alana were very popular kids and seemed to be invited to every social activity in the city. While Sherita was glad that her children had a positive and active social life, there were times when she felt like the dedicated chauffer for their increased calendar of events.

"Aight, Ma, we got it," insisted Josh, as he leaned forward to check his face in the rear-view mirror.

"Boy, move," shrieked Alana.

"Don't nobody care what you look like."

"Hey, hey, enough….now get out my car," Sherita said.

As the kids all filed out one-by-one, Sherita could hear the explosive sounds of the music coming from the gym and watched closely as students with bright colored jeans and extremely short skirts as clothing choices passed in front of the car. "Thank you, Ms. Coleman," Demetri said.

"You're welcome sweetie," Sherita replied, thinking, what a nice young man, if only her children had such manners.

The gym had been completely transformed to look like the inside of a nightclub. As the four entered the room, they immediately separated as if they had never even arrived in the same car.

"Oh my gosh, that's my song," blurted out Janet as she grabbed Alana's arm and made a mad dash for the dance floor. The DJ was playing the hit R&B throwback single "We Got Our Own Thing" by Heavy D and the Boys. A favorite of Alana's as well; she went willingly and

79

proceeded to do the latest dance moves with her friend. Alana enjoyed

hanging out with Janet. Janet always knew how to have a good time and

never really focused on what other people's thoughts were about her.

You either liked her or you didn't and Alana was OK with that. As DJ

Daze mixed in Guys "Groove Me" the girls instantly fell into the mood

of the environment. The room was dimly lit with the majority of the

lighting coming from a few strobe and track lights along the walls. It

was somewhat difficult to see people in the crowd. The whole school

had to be at this party or at least that is how it felt. The DJ slowed the

music down a bit to give the now sweaty group of high-strung kids a rest.

The chaperones and teachers decided to take the opportunity to enjoy a

song or two. Janet and Alana made their way off the dance floor and out

of nowhere, Josh runs up to Alana.

"Hey sis, I need two dollars," he said out of breath.

"Boy, what is wrong with you? And get off of me," she said.

"Come on Alana! I left my wallet at home and I need two dollars," he

pleaded again.

Clearly irritated at always needing to be responsible for her little brother,

Alana reached in her pocket and handed Josh a five dollar bill. Before she could read him the rules regarding her money, he snatched it out of her hand, yelled thanks and took off in the other direction. Rolling her eyes, she briefly looked down to put the items back in her pocket and as she turned slightly she bumped into Delton. "Hey Lan, what's up?" he asked with a smile on his face. Somewhat shocked to see him, she gently smiled back and replied, "hey, I'm sorry I guess I didn't see you standing there."

As she looked around, she had somehow lost sight of Janet in the midst of the conversation with Josh.

"Oh, no problem. You want to dance?" Delton asked.

"Sure," she said.

The two headed for the dance floor and as fate would have it Brandy's "Have You Ever," piped through the sound system and suddenly they seemed to be the only two people in the room.

Standing in line at the photo booth, Josh, tried desperately not to smile so much while standing there with Tracy.

"So, you really look pretty tonight," he said sweetly.

Smiling and looking at him shyly, her eyes were reminiscent of a word of thanks. "I am glad you decided to come to the dance Ms. Tracy, so I can see your cute face and maybe even get you to dance with me before the night is over."

"I told you earlier today that I was coming," Tracy said.

"I know, but you know, I was just excited about the anticipation of seeing you," he said.

"Oh, looks like we are next, here hold this for a minute."

Tracy handed Josh her purse as she held up a tiny mirror and lipstick case to fix her lip-gloss.

"You look adorable," he assured her as he grabbed her hand and they entered the booth. After a brief set of instructions by a gentleman who appeared to be the booth administrator, the two got in. Just like in the mall, the first photo was whacky and off guard, they laughed at it and immediately coordinated their efforts for the next one with Tracy sitting on Josh's lap and her arm around his neck. They smiled and were blinded by the bright flashing light, as the machine announced a one-minute warning to their last photo. Hurriedly discussing what to do next, in an instant, Josh reached over and kissed Tracy on the lips, just as the camera flashed. The two gazed into each other's eyes for what seemed like an eternity and they knew this was going to be a night to remember.

As the booth monitor ushered them out so the next set of horny teenagers could have their turn, the two waited off to the side for their pictures to print. As they stood there with anticipation, Josh grabbed Tracy by the hand.

"Look how cute these pictures are!" Tracy gushed.

"Yeah, lucky for you I was willing to be in them, huh," Josh said jokingly. Playfully punching his arm, she laughed at his arrogant sense of humor and put the pictures in her purse.

"Hey, hold on a minute, let me see'em real quick," Josh said.

Tracy handed one of the two strips of photos to Josh and they walked toward Alana and Delton standing by the door.

"Alana," Josh yelled out.

"Can you hold these for me? Put them in your purse til we get home," he said.

"I didn't bring a purse, and do I look like your personal assistant?" she asked irritated. Sucking his teeth, he handed the photos to his sister and she willfully complied. As they were all standing there, Josh realized that Delton was there as well.

"Delton," he asked with a shocked look on his face.

"Dude, where you been?"

Josh knew Delton very well, and had heard he and his family had moved back to Atlanta. This was his first time seeing him. The two embraced one another with the classic black man greeting and smiled pleasantly.

"Josh, man what's up?" Delton said.

"Dude, I heard you were back on the block man, good to see you. Yo, this is my girl Tracy. Tracy, this is my boy Delton, from back in the day and oh yeah, that's my sister Alana," he said.

As everyone provided their pleasantries to one another, Tracy indicated that she needed to get something to drink. Josh understood that to mean she was bored with hanging out with his sister, and gave his daps to everybody and the two walked off.

"Lil'Josh, check him out with a girlfriend," joked Delton. "Who knew he would actually grow up?"

"Don't let the smooth talk fool you," Alana said. The two chuckled at her comment and headed to find a seat to rest. As they found a table with a couple of empty chairs, Alana noticed Janet standing off to the side by herself.

"Janet, Janet!" Alana yelled over the loud music.

Clearly not hearing her, Alana walked over to her friend.

"Hey girl, where'd you run off to?" she asked.

"Looks like I should be asking you that question," Janet said with an attitude. Somewhat confused at Janet's response, she asked.

"Is everything OK?"

"Yeah, I am fine," Janet, replied with a dry tone.

"Well, Delton and I are sitting over here if you want to come and join us," Alana offered as she headed back to the table.

Glancing at the clock on the wall, Alana couldn't believe it was already 11:15 p.m. As she approached the table, she could see that Delton had walked away and so she sat down to wait. Within a few minutes he emerged with one hand behind his back.

"Hey, I thought you did a whodini on me," she said jokingly.

"You won't ever have to worry about that," he assured.

"Where'd you go?"

Smiling, Delton reveals a perfect single red rose from behind his back and leans over to present it to Alana. Looking up smiling and blushing, she gave him a puppy-dog look of happiness. Delton took that as the all clear to kiss her. Just as he leaned over to kiss Alana on the lips, Janet approached clearing her throat in disruption. Settling for a quick peck on the cheek, Delton stood back up and offered his seat next to Alana to Janet. Looking at the clock again, Alana knew it was time to round up her brother and his goofy friend so they could be out front to meet Sherita. Delton walked with Alana toward the car as the others raced along the sidewalk.

"I really enjoyed hanging out with you tonight Lan," Delton said. "Maybe if you are free this weekend we can catch a movie or something," he asked.

"Yeah, I would like that," she replied. Just give me a call tomorrow.

"Let's go ALANA," Josh was yelling annoyingly from the side of the car as if to embarrass her.

Laughing at his antic, the two hugged and Alana headed to get in the car and Delton disappeared into the crowd in the opposite direction. This would truly end up being a night to remember for Alana, the difference is, it wouldn't be because of the fun she had with Janet, but because of a new relationship with Delton.

Josh and Demetri chatted nonstop on the ride home, eagerly attempting to recap every memory of the night. However, the awkward silence between Alana and Janet set the tone for what would be an interesting

senior year in high school. Janet appeared visibly unnerved about

something, but rode in silence the rest of the way starring out the

window. Alana was exhausted. Her thoughts were still on Delton, she

figured whatever was bothering Janet, the two of them would sort it all

out tomorrow.

Chapter 11

The next several months played out like a well-written fairytale in the lives of the Coleman family members. As fall led into the holidays, the year seemed to be moving along quickly. Alana and Delton became an item after securing the lead roles in Romeo and Juliet. Josh and Tracy were enjoying the benefits of the puppy love atmosphere that surrounded their relationship. Sherita and Lamont had managed to find a common groove with one another that lent itself to an unexpected love affair that linked together the nerves of their hearts like chains never meant to be broken. The family was even adjusting to the news that Tyrone had proposed to his longtime girlfriend Nicole and planning a wedding in late summer.

This would prove to be a busy year for the family, one that would present itself with lots of unexpected challenges that would test their friendships, their faith, their love, their trust and that once common family bond that seemed so unshakable.

By the first week in June, the weather in Atlanta was hot and blazingly in full effect. With her daughter's high school graduation Friday and Nicole's bridal shower the next day, Sherita decided to take the week off and prepare for the whirlwind of emotions she was sure to experience this week. As she sat savoring the last sip of her morning coffee, she was startled by the sudden closeness of the warm lips that greeted her on the cheek.

"Good morning, Babe," whispered Lamont.

With an unexpected flinch and turn of her head, Sherita realized she had been daydreaming and didn't hear Lamont come down the stairs.

"Oh, good morning sweetie. Sorry, you startled me. I didn't hear you come down the stairs," she replied.

"Yeah, you looked like you were trying to solve the puzzle to world hunger in that head of yours. What's on your mind?"

As Lamont, pulled out a chair at the dining room table, Sherita got up to fix him a cup of coffee.

"Um, not much, I just know this is going to be an emotional week and I am just trying to mentally prepare myself for whatever, you know," she said as she throws her hands in the air with a sigh of frustration.

"Come on now Babe, don't go getting all emotional too soon, this is a happy week, and it is a normal feeling for a mother to be all jittery about her baby graduating from high school."

"I know, you're right, I am just getting myself all worked up too early in the game."

Sherita set the coffee mug down in front of Lamont and leaned over to kiss him on the forehead.

"So - what is on your agenda for today?" he asked.

"You took the entire week off and for the past four days I have left you here in the house in your pajamas and come back to that same look. What is the plan for today?" he asked sarcastically.

"Shut-up, Lamont and go to work," Sherita said with a chuckle.

"I am just taking full advantage of getting my rest and relaxation in a quiet house with you and the kids off at work and school every day.

"Hmmm," he replied with an eyebrow raised.

As he stood to put his cup in the sink, his cellphone started ringing. Lamont glanced down at the phone and quickly switched the sound to vibrate. With nervous inflection in his eyes, he walked toward Sherita grabbed her and pulled her close to his body. Rocking back and forth and gazing down into her eyes he leaned in to kiss her lips. What would have normally been a quick peck-and-go turned into a passionate kiss that felt like it lasted forever. Still standing with her eyes closed, Sherita

slowly looked up at Lamont and mouthed the words I love you.

He leaned in once again and with a quick peck said, "I love you, too."

Playfully slapping her on the butt he says, "I better go before you give

me a reason to call in sick today."

Flashing her beautiful smile, she says, "there would be no argument from

me Mr. Washington."

As he turned around to grab his coat and keys, his cellphone started

ringing again. Lamont hit the vibrate button once more and headed out

the door.

There was a lot that needed to be done today and Lamont was right,

Sherita had spent the majority of the week in the house and had not

accomplished anything. She had to get out of the house today and run

some errands. She needed to pick up the dry cleaning with Alana's dress

for tomorrow's ceremony. She still needed to shop for a bridal shower

gift for Nicole. What the hell do you buy the woman who is marrying

your ex-husband? She needed to finalize the plans for the restaurant

where the family would celebrate tomorrow night after the graduation.

Once Sherita got in the shower, she didn't hear the house phone ringing.

Focused on getting dressed and getting her day started, she never noticed

the voicemail message that was left. Looking at her watch, it was

already 11 a.m., and half the day had passed. Luckily, Tyrone bought a

car for Josh and Alana to share just before spring break and as a result

Sherita was officially off tour-bus duty in having to rush to pick them up

from school every day. The kids had managed to be quite responsible

with their newfound freedom, and Sherita and Tyrone were quite proud

of the two of them for not killing each other in the process.

Once at the mall, Sherita decided to stop in Frederick's of Hollywood.

What better way to show her support for Nicole and Tyrone than to help

spice things up in the bedroom for the two of them? "May I help you

find something?" asked the salesperson.

"Um, I am looking for a sexy bridal shower gift," she replied.

"OK, is this for yourself or a girlfriend of yours?"

With a light chuckle, Sherita was amused at the question, she hardly

thought of Nicole as her girlfriend, but hey, whatever.

"Um, sure, why not?" Sherita replied sarcastically.

The young lady pointed Sherita toward an array of brightly colored lingerie teddies. Realizing the store was hosting a phenomenal sale, Sherita thought what the hell, she may as well pick up a few items for her and Lamont to celebrate with as well. She selected a nice hot pink costume for Nicole and waited for the salesgirl to wrap it succinctly. Having spent way too much time in the mall, she realized that she really needed to step it up to finish her rounds. The kids would be home from school soon and she wanted to be there when they arrived.

Pulling up into the driveway, she realized they had already beat her home and judging by the additional car in the driveway, they had guests. As she walked in the door, she saw Alana and Delton sitting at the kitchen table and Josh sitting at a distance on the sofa.

"Mom! Guess what?" shouted Alana as she stood up from the table.

Startled at first, she wasn't sure if her daughter's mood was good or bad.

"What, sweetheart?"

"I got in, I got in!!"

Alana shouted to the top of her lungs jumping around in glee and excitement. Not really sure where she got into, Sherita just went with the flow of her daughters excitement.

"Got in where, honey?" she asked.

"NYU mom, NYU!!!"

"Oh, honey that is wonderful, I am so excited for you."

Since her 10th grade year when her dad took her on a weekend trip to visit New York University, Alana knew she wanted to attend the prestigious school and study drama.

"I need to call Daddy," Alana yelled as she snatched the cordless phone off the wall.

While Alana screamed uncontrollably on the phone with her dad, Josh walks up to Sherita standing nearly a foot taller than her, puts his arm around her shoulder and says, "looks like it will be just me and you, Mom."

With that thought, Sherita just glanced over at Delton and simultaneously leaned her head on her son's torso and said "looks like it son."

Chapter 12

Saturday morning had arrived, and Sherita laid in the bed staring at the ceiling recounting in her memory the events from the day before. With a warm smile across her face, she couldn't help but think of how proud she was of Alana and how excited she was for her to be able to attend the college she had worked so hard to get into. Alana had been accepted to six other schools, but had been anxiously holding out hope that NYU would come through. Rolling over, she realized that Lamont was up and out early this morning. Not giving it a second thought, she immediately turned her attention to figuring out which of her friends she could convince to go with her to Nicole's bridal shower later that evening. Sherita decided to call Kendra.

"Maybe I should just move in with you guys, and that way it would eliminate all this early Saturday morning calling shit you seem to keep inflicting upon me," Kendra said sarcastically as she answered the phone. Laughing out loud, Sherita realized it was 8 o'clock in the morning and apologized to her best friend. "Girl, get yo'ass up. You don't need to be sleep this late no way, we got stuff to do," Sherita said jokingly.

"What the hell kind of stuff I got to do today?" Kendra asked.

"Well, for starters, you need to figure out what you are going to wear tonight for this bridal shower WE are attending for Nicole."

"Ni'who?" Kendra said with a slight shriek in her voice.

"Nicole. Girl, she invited me to her bridal shower tonight and I couldn't say no," Sherita said.

"Hell, but I can," joked Kendra.

"Come on Kendra, I can't go by myself, that would just be awkward," Sherita pleaded.

"No what's awkward, is this incestuous relationship you and Tyrone have managed to maintain all these damn years, and somehow you have hypnotized the people you're fucking to believe that this shit is normal. Hell that's what is awkward?" Kendra said.

Laying there with a plastered smile on her face, Sherita was quite amused at her friend's blunt honesty when it came to her and Tyrone. Sherita and Tyrone had managed to seemingly engage all the people they dated over the years into their lives without cause, but this was different, he was actually going to marry this chick. At first, Sherita had to admit she was bit taken aback that day that Tyrone invited her to lunch to share his plan of proposal to Nicole. Sherita always knew that once the kids got old enough to be comfortable with their separate relationships that surely something like this was bound to happen, but she just hadn't factored in a viable response. Yelling in the phone at this point, Kendra says, "what the hell time is this damn shower Sherita?"

"7:00 o'clock," Sherita said in a calm thank-you-so-very-much voice. With a loud sigh in the phone, Kendra reluctantly agreed to attend. At the end of the day, Sherita was her girl and she would never let her enter enemy territory alone.

"Pick me up at 6:30," she said and abruptly hung up the phone. Pulling the phone away from her ear and looking at it in disbelief that she hung up, Sherita put the phone back on the base, got out the bed and headed for the bathroom.

Not hearing the phone ringing while in the bathroom, just as she turned off the water the phone stopped and Sherita proceeded with her morning. Walking through the house, she realized it was silent and wondered where everyone was. Looking out the window in the kitchen, she saw that the kids' car was gone, but noticed that Lamont's car was still in the driveway.

Hearing the muffled sounds of conversation on the porch, she headed toward the door. As she approached the door, she overheard Lamont on the phone in what sounded like an intense conversation. Hearing him say sternly to the other person on the other end, that "this shit is over," Sherita decided not to open the door, but instead tiptoed hurriedly back to the room as she realized he was turning the knob to enter the house. Emerging from the hallway as if it were her first time out of the room, she entered the kitchen intentionally walking over the exact boards in the floor that would squeak to announce her presence. Lamont turned around from the sink to face her and smiled as she headed toward him.

"Hey babe, good morning," he said as he reached out to pull her close for a hug and kiss.

"Good morning to you, too. You're up early," she inquired.

"Yeah, I got up and watched some *Sports* Center for a bit this morning. You were sleeping so well, I just didn't want to bother you," he said.

"Oh, I see, where are the kids?" she asked.

"Well, Delton came to take Alana to breakfast about 20 minutes ago and Josh went to go wash the car and get an oil change, he said his dad had scheduled the appointment for this morning," he replied.

"Oh yeah, that is right, I forgot Tyrone mentioned that last night at the party." Reaching over to pull Sherita close to him again, he proceeded to kiss her passionately. The business of the past few weeks had them both missing each other daily. Lamont had been spending an innate amount of time at the office and Sherita was planning for Alana's graduation, all of which had put their relationship on the back burner. Giving into his advances, Sherita went along with his lead as he picked her up and headed back down the hallway to the bedroom. With her legs wrapped around his waist, Lamont quickly closed the door to the room, as he gently laid her down on the bed and proceeded to kiss her neck and made his way down her body. Lamont was madly in love with Sherita and would do anything in the world for her. He had never had a woman like her and he didn't plan on letting anything or anyone ruin their relationship. As the intensity of the moment continued to build between the two of them, they both took their time exploring one another's bodies for the ultimate level of ecstasy. It had been awhile since the two made love and it was clear that their bodies were ready to explode. Sherita loved Lamont and she loved being with him, but the past few weeks he had been a bit distant and she knew that eventually she would have to get to the bottom of it. However, right now she chose to bask in the moment

of bliss that would satisfy her innermost desires.

Chapter 13

IHOP was extremely crowded that morning and it seemed like Delton and Alana had waited in line forever to be seated. Once they were able to place their order, Alana knew that it was going to be difficult to share her thoughts with Delton about the future of their relationship.

"So, cool party last night, huh?" she asked, trying to get the conversation going. "Yeah, your mom and dad really are proud of you Lan."

"Yeah, it's just weird to think in less than two months we will be off in college," she said. "I mean, you're going to be at UGA and me in New York, it will be a whole new world."

"Yeah, I've been thinking about that," Delton said.

"Alana, I know how much you want to go to NYU and I certainly want to see your dreams come true, so, I was thinking that maybe after my first semester at Georgia, that I could look into transferring to NYU so we can be together."

Suddenly not hungry anymore, Alana realized that now was as good a time as any to tell Delton how she felt about their relationship. The past year had been a great year, but she realized that, while she cared for Delton a lot, she had no intentions on spending the rest of her life with him. However, it was evident that his thoughts were completely different.

"Delton, we need to talk," she said with a sigh.

As Alana braced herself for the conversation, the waitress delivered the food to the table.

"Hold that thought Lan, lets pray," he said.

As the two grabbed hands, Delton began to pray out loud.

"Lord, we come to you this morning to say thank you for bringing me and Alana together and for making this past year the best year of my life. Lord, we thank you for both of us getting accepted into college and for keeping us close as we separate in the fall. Oh, yeah and thank you Lord for this food, Amen."

Slightly rolling her eyes in the back of her head, Alana sat back in the booth to brace herself.

"Delton, I want to break-up," she blurted out before she realized it.

Delton dropped his silverware on the table in shock and stared at Alana from across the table with a look of confusion.

"What?" he asked with a look of building rage.

"Look, Del, I think you are an amazing guy and I have had a wonderful time over the past year, spending time with you and hanging out and stuff. But I got to admit, that I really don't want to go off to school with a boyfriend in another state."

"That's why I am going to transfer," he pleaded.

"You aren't hearing me Delton, I don't want to go off to school with a boyfriend. Look, it will be a whole new world, new environment for both of us and we need to be free to explore everything that freshman explore in college. I am sorry to have to tell you like this, but I just didn't know how else to share it with you. I still want us to be friends and to keep in touch, but I just think that we need to end it on a positive note instead of trying to maintain a long-distance relationship."

Completely in disagreement with what was taking place, Delton knew that it didn't make much sense trying to talk Alana out of this decision. He felt as if his heart had been handed to him on a platter. Visibly upset, he nervously reached into his pocket in search of his car keys. He incidentally ran his hand across the small jewelry box in his pocket with the gold locket he had just purchased for Alana. He was planning on giving it to her at breakfast with a photo of the two of them inside.

Fighting back tears, Delton got up from the table and walked out of the restaurant. Assuming that he was just going to sit in the car, Alana waited a few minutes before signaling for the waitress's attention for the check.

"Is everything alright?" inquired the waitress, noticing that neither of them had touched their food.

"Yeah, everything is fine," Alana, said with a sad sigh.

"May I have the check please?"

Once she paid the bill, she headed out the door of the restaurant. Delton, was gone, it appeared as though he had left her. Pissed, she thought, to herself she couldn't blame him, he was devastated. She reached in her purse for her cellphone to call Josh.

"YO!" Josh yelled in the phone with loud music from EPMD blaring in the background.

"Josh, where are you?" Alana asked in a calm voice.

Immediately realizing something was wrong with his sister, Josh turned the music down in the car.

"What's wrong Alana?" he asked with concern.

"Can you come pick me up, please? I am at the IHOP around the corner from our house," she said. Hearing his sister's silent sniffles in the phone, he immediately turned the car around to head to her rescue.

"Aight, I will be there in five minutes."

As Alana stood out front, she could hear the roar of her brother's music long before she saw the car. She quickly wiped her eyes to dismiss any signs of tears and got in the car. Turning the music off at this point, Josh pulled into a vacant parking space and turned to look at his big sister.

"Ok, what is going on? Are you pregnant?"

"What!"

"No!"

"I am not pregnant idiot," she said as she pushed her brother's arm.

"Whew, good, cause I was 'bout to say, I don't want to be in the room when you tell Mommy and Daddy that news," Josh said jokingly.

"I broke up with Delton and he was upset and left the restaurant," she said. "What? He left you up here and went home to cry like a little punk? What kind of shit is that?" Josh said angrily.

"Josh, he was upset, I guess I deserved it," she said.

"You don't ever deserve some dude leaving you in no restaurant because his dumb ass can't handle rejection. He better be glad I wasn't here."

As Josh started the car back up, he reached over to turn up the music, and looked at his sister.

"Why'd you break up with him?"

"I don't want a long-distance relationship in college," she said as she stared straight ahead.

Shaking his head in agreement, he leaned over to his sister and turned her face toward his and said, "that was the best thing." He leaned their foreheads up against each other and said, "you gone be alright Sis." Alana smiled at her little brother realizing she just might miss him when she goes off to school. The two headed home.

As they arrived at the house, it appeared as though Sherita and Lamont were still at home. Alana and Josh entered the house through the garage as the phone was ringing off the hook. Alana reached to grab it and the male voice on the other end asked to speak with Sherita Coleman. Alana indicated that she was unavailable and asked if there was a message. The gentleman indicated that the call was of a private matter and that he would try back later. Knocking on the door to her mom's room, she could hear Sherita yell, just a minute. Instantly realizing why they needed the minute and why the door was closed and locked, Alana was sick to her stomach.

She yelled, "never mind," and headed to her room.

Alana stared at the ceiling as she laid across the bed thinking about her encounter with Delton. She knew in her heart that it was the right thing to do. And besides Delton could be a bit clingy at times and she just didn't want to be restricted while away at college. She really did hope that one day he would be able to forgive her and perhaps they could be friends. Although she knew that day wouldn't be soon.

Chapter 14

Sherita pulled up in Kendra's driveway at 6:25 p.m. She called her friend to let her know that she was outside in the car.

"Yeah, yeah, I am coming," Kendra, said answering the phone.

Sherita hung up and did a quick once over of herself in the vanity mirror. Deciding to touch up her lip-gloss, she felt cute and sexy. As Kendra made her way down the driveway, Sherita commented on her friend's outfit.

"Look at you, sexy momma, I like those jeans," she complimented. Doing a quick model pose in front of the car, Kendra smiled glowingly as she revealed a form-fitting pair of dark-washed flared Levi jeans, a canary yellow one-sleeve halter-top and a gorgeous pair of gold Gucci stilettos. Kendra was a beautiful woman; her caramel-colored skin and perfectly straight white teeth were the icing on the cake to her perfect size 10, 5'4" body type with a sister-girl ass. She wore her black shoulder-length hair in a curly style that complemented the dimples in her face. Blowing the horn in agreement, Kendra, laughed out loud as she got in the car. Leaning over to hug and greet her friend, she complimented Sherita as well.

"Look at you, lady in white," said Kendra in awe of Sherita's outfit.

"Yeah, well, you know, I figured I would remind her who the original Mrs. Coleman truly is," she said jokingly.

"So, where is this damn shower and how long do we have to stay?" inquired Kendra sarcastically.

"Girl, she is having it at the Ritz Carlton Buckhead Hotel and we won't need to be there any longer than an hour and a half. I was thinking afterward, maybe we could head over to Twist for a drink."

Just as the conversation was getting started Sherita's phone rang.

"Hello," she said.

"Hey, it's me," Tyrone said.

A bit surprised, Sherita turned the music down.

"Hey Tyrone, what's up? Is everything OK?"

"Yeah, I was just calling to say thank you for being so cool with this whole marriage thing. It really means a lot to me that you are OK with it and being supportive," he said.

"Tyrone, I told you that I was OK with you and Nicole getting married and I am truly happy for you. You deserve this, she loves you and it seems like you love her, right?"

"Yeah, yeah, no doubt, I do, but you know I don't ever want to be disrespectful to you or your feelings."

"Well, thanks for the thought, but I am fine."

"As a matter of fact, Kendra and I are headed to the bridal shower as we speak." "It's not too late to change your mind Ty," Kendra yelled jokingly from the passenger side of the car.

"Tell big head I said what's up," he replied.

"Ok, well, you two have fun and hey...behave," he said sarcastically.

"Seriously, you're telling me to behave," she said.

"Ahh, yeah, with you and Killa-brotha-quick Kendra, I should probably send some undercover guards," he laughed.

"Whatever boy, bye."

As the two pulled up to the valet at the Ritz, Kendra said she was getting out and running in to use the restroom while Sherita took care of the car. Sherita agreed and offered to meet her in the lobby. Upon entering the lobby, Sherita noticed a nice crowd of people. Not sure who was there for what, she decided to grab a seat and wait on Kendra. As she scanned the room to find a visible spot to chill, she caught the eye of a very handsome stranger sitting with a group of equally attractive men.

110

"*Hmmm they must be having the 'Fine Ass Brothers Convention' here today*," she thought to herself. Sherita smiled politely and turned to see if her friend was anywhere in sight. As Kendra approached, Sherita stood up nervously, and she could feel the piercing eyes of the handsome gentleman from across the room. "Damn, girl, I didn't realize you looked this hot," Kendra said.

"Huh," Sherita said with a look of confusion.

"I said, damn, I like that outfit you got on."

"Surely if Tyrone seen you tonight he would be reconsidering his marriage to the librarian-looking chick."

"Kendra, she is not a librarian," Sherita said.

"Well, whatever, she just homely looking if you ask me."

Sherita did feel extremely sexy all of a sudden as she made her way across the hotel lobby in her skin-tight white Dolce and Gabana skinny leg jeans, white flowy top that revealed just enough cleavage, and shoes and accessories to match. Sherita's size 6 frame was not to be ignored by men and women alike. She always commanded the attention in a room, with her powerful beauty, yet confident spirit. "Girl, did you

111

notice the group of guys sitting over in the corner," Kendra asked as the two headed toward the ballroom.

"Yeah, I did, wonder where they are from?" Sherita questioned.

"I don't know, but I tell you what, if this bunch of bridal bitches aren't as entertaining as I think they need to be, sweetie, I will be able to give you a run down on every brother over there before the end of the night," Kendra joked. "Well let's hope you don't have to be inspector gadget today," Sherita joked.

The room was elegantly decorated in soft pastel colors with hints of silver.

"This shit looks like Easter," whispered Kendra.

Trying desperately not to bust out laughing, Sherita smiled politely said hello to everyone she made eye contact with in passing in the room. Although she had to admit, Kendra was right, the decoration in the room was a bit bunny festive. As she approached a group of women standing and chatting, she lightly touched Nicole on the shoulder. When Nicole turned around, she was pleasantly surprised to see Sherita and greeted her with a wide smile and open arms for a hug. "Sherita! So glad you made it." Nicole shrieked out loud.

"Oh, no problem. Thanks for inviting me," Sherita said.

Sherita reintroduced Nicole to Kendra and congratulated Nicole on the beautiful ballroom and decorations.

"Thank you so much again for coming Sherita, it really means a lot to me," she said nervously.

"I wouldn't have missed it for the world," chimed Sherita.

"Few more weeks until the big day, huh?" Sherita said.

"Yeah, it is coming quicker than I thought," Nicole replied with an excited look on her face.

"Oh! Come with me, I have someone I would like you to meet." Grabbing Sherita's hand, Nicole guided the ladies through the crowd to meet her mom and her sister.

"Sherita this is my mom Gladys and my sister Sheryl. Ladies this is Sherita, Josh and Alana's mom."

"Oh yes, very nice to meet you," Sheryl said forcibly.

Extending her hand to greet the two women, Sherita could feel them sizing her up. "Um, this is my best friend Kendra," Sherita immediately interjected while grabbing Kendra's hand.

"How nice of you both to come," Gladys said. "Your children are absolutely adorable, and very well-mannered."

"Thank you," Sherita said. "I appreciate that. They are great kids."

As she turned to face Nicole, she said she and Kendra would be sitting at a nearby table. Headed back toward the center of the room Sherita could feel her cellphone buzzing at the bottom of her purse.

"I don't know about you, but I felt like the sister was staring a bit too hard at your boobs, you don't think she on the other team, do you?" Kendra asked.

Halfway laughing, Sherita gave Kendra a "stop it" look as she answered the phone. "Hello," she said.

"I'm just saying," Kendra continued.

Straining to hear initially, she put her finger in her free ear to help block out the background noise.

"Hello," she asked again.

"Hello, is this Sherita Coleman?" asked the male voice on the other end of the phone.

"Yes, yes this is Sherita Coleman, how may I help you?"

With a look of concern on her face, Sherita wasn't quite sure why she would be receiving this type of call at 7:30 on a Saturday night. She motioned to Kendra that she would be right back.

"Hold on one moment please."

She decided to step out into the lobby so she could hear a little better.

"Hello? Thank you, I'm sorry. Who is this again?" Sherita asked.

"Ms. Coleman this is Dr. John Altman over at Piedmont Hospital, we have your sister here in the intensive care unit and we need for you to come to the hospital as quickly as possible."

Now nervous and confused, Sherita was trying to understand what was going on. She has just seen her older sister Belinda two days ago and she looked fine and she wasn't sure what was going on.

"Excuse me," she asked in a panic.

"Is Belinda alright?"

"I'm sorry Ms. Coleman, but it is not your sister Belinda that I am calling about, we have your other sister Allison here and she is in very serious condition," he said. "We really need you to come to the hospital as soon as possible, we just don't have a whole lot of time left."

"Allison?" Sherita said with question. "Umm, yes, sir. OK – I will be there as soon as I can, where is she again?"

"Piedmont Hospital, intensive care unit – please just ask for me when you get here," he said.

"Alright. Thank you, Dr. Altman I should be there within the hour." Sherita stood in the lobby with a dazed look on her face. Her mind wandered back to the message that Allison had left on her voicemail sometime last year. Sherita never called back and figured that Allison had moved on as well when she didn't hear back from her. What could be wrong and why would they be calling her from the hospital? As the flow of thoughts poured into her head, she was instantly distracted by a male voice with an accent.

"Excuse me," said the stranger. "Is everything alright?"

As Sherita looked up, she peered into the eyes of the very handsome gentleman she had exchanged glances with from the lobby earlier. She snapped back to reality, and said "no, not that I know of." Recognizing that perhaps she needed to sit down, he gently grabbed her by her elbow and guided her to the nearest vacant seat.

"Here, sit down for a minute," he said.

"You look like you need to take a quick rest. I don't know what that call was about, but I can say to you that no matter what it is, God will work it out."

"Thank you," she said.

"Sit here for a minute, I am going to get you some water," he said. Sherita complied. As he made his way back, he had a glass of ice water with a napkin and a straw. Sherita took a couple of sips and look relieved.

"Kroy," he said, extending his hand.

With a smile, she said, "Sherita."

"Very nice to meet you Ms. Sherita," he said jokingly in this amazingly sexy foreign-accented voice.

"May I say to you that you are an amazingly beautiful woman," he complimented. "Thank you," Sherita said blushing.

"You aren't half-bad yourself," she joked while taking a quick sip of the water. "Feeling better now?" he asked smiling.

"Yes, thank you, I just got some disturbing news and unfortunately I am going to have to leave to head to the hospital to check on a friend."

"Oh no, sorry to hear that, I pray everything works out," he said with a look of sincere concern on his face.

"Yeah, me, too," she said as she stood to head back into the ballroom.

"Um, thank you for the water. I better head back inside," she said.

"Listen, I am in town for a few days for work, I would love an opportunity to buy you coffee or lunch," he asked.

"Um, sure – I didn't bring my purse with me or I would give you a card," she said. "I will just put your number in my phone," he said.

"OK." The two exchanged numbers.

Sherita watched as Kroy put her number in his phone and he wrote his information on the napkin that came with the water.

"Great," he said.

The two exchanged pleasantries once again and Sherita headed back into the party to get Kendra. Upon entering the room, she could see that Kendra seemed to be enjoying herself as she had managed to make her way to the dance floor to join in on the electric slide. As the song's narrator instructed the crowd to "set it off on the left," Kendra was working it out on the dance floor. After waving her hands in the air, Sherita managed to get her friend's attention, and motioned for her to exit the floor. Still bopping to the music, Kendra could tell something was wrong by the look on Sherita's face.

"Sherita, girl, what's wrong?" asked Kendra as she grabbed her purse from the chair. "You look like somebody died."

"It's Allison, she is in intensive care at Piedmont and the doctor said that I am listed as next of kin and need to get there as quickly as possible," Sherita explained.

"Allison?" Kendra questioned.

Instantly concerned, Kendra complied and figured she would keep her comments to herself until after they knew what was going on. Sherita found Nicole and apologized for needing to leave and thanked her again for the invite. She assured Nicole that she would be at the wedding in a couple of weeks and told her to call her if she needed anything before then. Nicole understood and sent well wishes to Sherita's sick friend. As the two made their way out of the ball room, Kroy approached and told Sherita he had taken the liberty of having the valet pull her car around for her. She thanked him for his thoughtfulness and she and Kendra headed for the door.

"Ok, because I know you are distraught right now I am going to save my questions regarding the Latin heartthrob until later," she said.

"Get in the car, Kendra," Sherita insisted.

Her mind was racing a mile a minute, trying to understand what could be wrong. Whatever it was, she needed to brace herself for it. As Sherita whisked her way down Peachtree Street headed to Piedmont, she only knew one thing to do...pray.

Chapter 15

"How may I help you?"

Asked the lady at the desk, never taking her eyes off of the chart she was writing in.

"Um, yes my name is Sherita Coleman, I am here to see Dr. Altman."

"Ma'am what is the patient's name?"

"Allison, um, Allison Ellis," Sherita replied nervously.

"Ms. Ellis is in the ICU area located on the second floor. Take the elevator up, exit to your left and wait in the waiting area near the vending machines. I will call up and let Dr. Altman know you are there and someone will come get you." Following the instructions given, Sherita and Kendra headed anxiously to the elevator. Within minutes of waiting, a small framed, short white male doctor emerged from behind the double doors.

"Ms. Coleman," he asked looking at the two women.

"Yes, that is me," Sherita said as she extended her hand to greet Dr. Altman. "Thank you for coming. I tell you, you are a hard person to reach Ms. Coleman, I have tried your home phone several times over the past week or so and finally was able to track down a work number and your assistant reluctantly gave me your cell," he said with a persed smile.

"My apologies sir, if I had known you were trying to reach me, I would have certainly replied sooner," she said.

Let's have a seat for a minute and talk and then we can go back to see your sister. "Is this another family member," he asked looking at Kendra.

"Yes," Sherita replied abruptly before Kendra could respond.

"Ms. Coleman, I don't know how much you are aware of, but your sister is gravely ill. She is suffering with a rare skin disease call Scleroderma. She has been battling this disease for a few years now and has managed up to this point to do quite well. However, as with most cases of this debilitating disease, it eventually attacks the body's immune system and slowly proceeds to shut down vital organs. Unfortunately, once the liver is impacted, there really isn't much more that can be done and the end result is not favorable. Your sister is currently at that stage. She has been in and out of the hospital several times over the past year and this last time she has been here the better part of a week or so, which is when we started calling you. She is currently in a coma and unable to communicate, but she insisted up to the point that she could speak that we contact you should something happen indicating that you would be able to take care of everything."

As Sherita and Kendra sat with tears in their eyes, it was all just so much information to take in at one time.

"Do you have any questions Ms. Coleman," asked Dr. Altman.

Wiping away tears on the back of her hand.

"Um, how did this happen? How'd she get this Scler'whatever?" Sherita inquired, trying to find the words.

"Well, it is a degenerative disease and unfortunately, it is in the family gene pool. The uniqueness about it is that only one in every one thousand people are diagnosed each year and the majority of those impacted are women between the ages of 25 and 35. Your sister was diagnosed about eight years ago and believe it or not has done remarkably well up to this point. She managed to keep up with her physical activity, she has a beautiful and healthy 7-year-old daughter."

"Wait, did you say – daughter?" Sherita asked with question on her face.

"Why, yes – she defied the odds when she decided to go through with the pregnancy. By all accounts her body should not have been able to handle it, but she miraculously made it through."

With a deep sigh and resting her head in her hands she looked at Kendra for some sort of answer to it all. Kendra's look of shock on her face provided the only response that either of them had at the time, one of fear and despair.

"Can I see her?" Sherita asked.

"Yes," he replied. Kendra and Sherita stood at the same time, encompassing one another in a long hug of support.

"You can do this," whispered Kendra to Sherita.

"I will be right beside you the entire time."

The walk down the hall seemed endless. As they approached ICU room 13A, a sunken feeling overcame Sherita as she peered through the glass window at her friend lying motionless in the hospital bed. The nurses instructed the ladies to put on protective gear and gloves before entering the room. As they entered the room, the not so silent sounds of the breathing machine and monitoring instruments created what seemed like a well-orchestrated symphony. Sherita stood over the bed glaring down at Allison. Although slightly darker in color, Allison pretty much looked like herself. Sherita reached over and ran her hand over her friend's hair. "Hey Ally," she said softly.

"It's me Sher, I am here. I am so sorry I wasn't here sooner, but I am here now and I am not going anywhere. I spoke with Dr. Altman and he has given me a crash update on the events of your life over the past eight years. I can't believe it's been that long. I really wish you could talk to me and tell me what I can do to help. I hope you know that no matter what, I never stopped loving you and caring for you."

As Sherita searched for the words to say, she stood holding her friend's hand. As the nurse came in to check her vitals, Sherita felt what appeared to be a slight movement in Allison's hand.

"Oh my God, I think she just squeezed my hand," Sherita said with excitement as she wiped tears with the other one.

"Yeah, she probably did," confirmed the nurse. It isn't uncommon for patients in a coma to hear what's going on around them, they are just not able to respond in the manner they want to so that the family knows they hear them," she explained. "Does that mean there is a possibility she will get better?" inquired Sherita. "Anything is possible," said the nurse optimistically.

"Only time will tell. Can I get you ladies anything?" she asked.

"No thank you," they both said simultaneously.

"Alright, well I am right out front if you need anything," she said as she pulled the door slightly closed behind her.

As Kendra sat in shock, Sherita stood staring at her sick friend helplessly. Remembering the first day she met Allison years ago, the two became instant friends. It was almost as if God meant for them to be together. Allison had just moved to Atlanta from Ohio and Sherita was feeling her way through adulthood after leaving college the first year. The two became roommates and shared numerous memories and dreams in the years ahead. Allison actually taught Sherita how to drive a stick shift car in the middle of Joseph E. Lowery Boulevard in the West End. Smiling at the thought, Sherita remembered Allison's infectious laugh and how she would wake her up in the middle of the night wanting Sherita to sing to her. She loved Sherita's voice and always chastised her for not sharing her gift with the world. In that moment, Sherita sang a Whitney Houston classic called "Count On Me" and waited on God.

Count on me through thick and thin, a friendship that will never end. When you are weak, I will be strong, helping you to carry on. Call on me I will be there, don't be afraid. Please believe me when I say count on me...

As Sherita's voice carried throughout the room and into the hallway, a small crowd of nurses, doctors and others visiting in the unit peered through the door and window seeking a quick glance at the woman with the angelic voice, offering such a moving tribute to her loved one. Kendra wept silently in the chair, realizing that Sherita would never be the same after this. Maybe she should have supported Sherita's decision to return Allison's call last year. Perhaps she was being a bit to judgmental about Allison at the time. However, now it may be too late. Allison just may die.

Chapter 16

The next several weeks proved to be grueling on Sherita. She spent every moment she had at the hospital at Allison's bedside in hopes that her friend would open her eyes and speak to her. Sherita felt as though she was running out of time. Her life had all of a sudden taken on new meaning since learning of Allison's illness. She managed to be there in support of Tyrone and Nicole's wedding. The ceremony was lovely and Tyrone seemed happy. Josh and Alana were happy for their dad, but they were also worried about their mom.

Sherita was determined to spend some time with Alana this week. Tyrone and Nicole had been away on their honeymoon and she felt bad that the kids were somewhat fending for themselves. Alana would be leaving for school in a few weeks and Sherita really hadn't done enough to help her prepare for her big move to New York. Alana and Josh both were very understanding about the situation with Allison. They, too, were devastated when they heard the news. Allison had always been like an aunt to them and it pained them both to see their mother sad. The long days and nights had also taken a toll on Sherita's relationship with Lamont. She was up early most days and out the house before he was and barely made it home for dinner at night. Dealing with his own set of issues, Lamont hadn't been spending as much time at the house as usual. The two of them had separated from one another deciding that they needed to give their relationship a rest. He attempted a couple of times to sit with Sherita at the hospital, but with his own issues looming, he posed more of an uncomfortable distraction than anything. There were some things going on that he needed to straighten out and he wasn't ready to involve Sherita at this point. And besides, with all that she was dealing with regarding her friend, he didn't want to give her more reason to worry. Meanwhile, in the time that Sherita had been at the hospital, she had managed to meet Allison's 7-year-old daughter, Luckye, and shared a few brief moments with her. Luckye was staying with her father in the upper north side of Atlanta and they only made it to the hospital once or twice a week. Luckye was a beautiful girl, every bit the spitting image of her mother. She was very aware of what was going on, indicating that Allison had told her all about life and death and assuring her that there was nothing to be afraid of. As Sherita sat flipping through the channels on the TV, she realized she needed to get home to meet the kids for dinner. It was nearing 6 o'clock, she didn't want to disappoint

Josh and Alana, and she really missed them. As she stood to put on her coat, she walked over to kiss Allison on her forehead and the nurse walked in.

"Ms. Coleman," she said.

"Dr. Altman would like to speak with you for a minute, if you have time."

Sherita nodded her head in agreement, gathered her things and followed the young lady down the hall to a small cubbyhole of an office where Dr. Altman was reviewing charts. He stood to greet her.

"Ms. Coleman, thank you for coming, I am so glad I caught you here visiting today."

"Yes, I have been here so much lately, I feel like I should be collecting a check," she said jokingly.

"Yeah, well, that is understandable, most families get to that point," he replied.

As Sherita sat down, she somehow knew that this conversation would not be good. "Ms. Coleman, as you know, your sister's condition has not changed in a manner that is being helpful to her quality of life. She and I have had numerous discussions surrounding what would happen or need to happen in the event that we got to this particular stage in her treatment and care," he continued. Currently, she is being kept alive by the life-support machine that she is on and really not showing any signs of the ability to breathe on her own. She indicated early on, that she did not want to be kept alive by machines past so many days and unfortunately, we have reached that point. With you being listed as next of kin, we will need your consent to carry out her final wishes."

Feeling as if she were all of a sudden in a bad episode of a Charlie Brown movie, Sherita had to force her brain to take it all in and comprehend the information. "So, you want me to pull the plug on her, is that what you're telling me?" she asked with a look of confusion. "Unfortunately, Ms. Coleman, it is time that we carry out her wishes," he replied. Dr. Altman handed Sherita a large manila envelope.

"She asked that I give this to you in the event that we got to this point. I do not know what is inside of it, but I will assume that it may be pertinent information regarding her final wishes and arrangements. Why don't you go home and speak with your family and tomorrow you and I can meet to discuss the final decision." As Dr. Altman stood up, so did Sherita. In shock, she reached for the envelope and headed down the hall toward the elevator. Sherita drove with tears streaming down her face, she was afraid to look inside the envelope, as she already knew what the expectations inside would be. She prayed out loud asking God for His guidance and His strength to do the right thing.

"Lord, I need you now more than ever," she prayed.

"Please, Lord, give me a sign of what is the right thing to do."

As she pulled into the driveway, she realized she needed to pull herself together. Wiping her tear-stained face, she got out of the car and headed inside. She still had all intentions on going to dinner with her family and right now, she needed them like never before. However, when she got out of the car, she saw Lamont standing on the porch talking on his cellphone. As she approached the front steps, he abruptly ended his call and greeted her with a hug.

"Hey babe," he said. "You're home early tonight, is everything alright?" he asked. Needing to feel his heartbeat, she just fell into his open arms and buried her head in his chest and breathed a sigh of despair.

Realizing that she has been through a lot, he complied and stood in silence holding the love of his life in his arms and gently rocking her back and forth with comfort. After a few minutes, she lifted her head, reached up to give him a kiss on the lips and headed inside. Although

things had been a bit rocky between them lately, Sherita was glad to

know he was still being supportive.

"Hey Ma," Josh said as Sherita and Lamont came in the house.

"How's Aunt Ally today, she any better?" he inquired.

"No, son, Aunt Ally isn't any better and unfortunately, she isn't going to

be," she replied with a sigh.

"Ahh man, sorry to hear that Ma," Josh replied.

"Where is Alana?" she asked.

"She is upstairs in her room. Are we still going to dinner?"

"Yes, yes we are, so go get ready so that we can head out," she said with

a smile. Leaning over to kiss his mother's cheek, Josh did as he was

instructed. Lamont's cellphone started ringing. Sherita, walked down

the hall to the bedroom to give him his privacy, with all that she was

dealing with she didn't have time to play detective with Lamont today.

She put her things on the bed and decided she would wait until later to

open the envelope. Tonight was about her kids and she was going to

make sure the focus stayed on them. Sherita changed her shoes and

splashed some cold water on her face. She yelled up the stairs for the kids to come down and she headed toward the kitchen. Lamont was standing at the sink and turned and indicated that he was going to have to miss dinner, he had an important business meeting that had just come up and he needed to head out. A bit upset at this sudden revelation, Sherita was determined not to let anything take away this time with her kids. She looked at him with a blank stare and just headed out the door to the car. On the drive over, Sherita decided to catch up with what was going on in the lives of her children. The past two weeks literally seemed like two months and she felt extremely out of touch.

"So, Lan, I haven't seen Delton around the house lately, is everything going OK with you two?" she asked.

"Mom, you haven't been around the house lately, so you haven't seen anyone," Alana replied sarcastically.

With a light chuckle, she gave her daughter a look of agreeance and continued the conversation.

"Ok, so you got me on that, but what's up?"

"Well, Mom, I broke up with Delton a couple weeks ago," Alana, said with a sad undertone.

"Oh no, honey, I'm sorry, what happened?" Sherita asked with a look of concern on her face.

"I just felt like it was time, and I didn't want to put myself in a position of trying to maintain a long-distance relationship while in college. I mean, I really want to be able to experience new people and things during my freshman year and just not be constrained with a boyfriend, you know?" Alana rambled on and on as if she were still trying to convince herself that it was the right thing to do.

"Well, Lan, I think that was a very mature decision to make and you're right, freshman year is a big deal and you will be meeting lots of new people and experiencing new things. Are you sure you are OK with your decision?" Sherita asked. "Yeah, I am OK with it," Alana said with a sigh.

"How did Delton take it?"

"Delton won't speak to me, he hasn't returned any of my calls since that day. I would like to be his friend, but, I can't chase him to make that work," she said. "Well honey, just give him some time, I am sure he will come around. You still have a couple more weeks before you leave.

135

Surely he will reach out to you in that time. Boys are very different than girls when it comes to relationships," Sherita said.

"Trust me it doesn't get any easier as you get older."

Sherita was very proud of her daughter for recognizing the need to expand her horizons. She and Tyrone had discussed how to handle the whole Delton relationship once Alana went off to college anyway. The two were starting to think that he was a bit too clingy with Alana. As fate would have it, it worked itself out. One less thing to worry about, Sherita thought to herself. Sherita was glad she took the time to have dinner with the kids. She did feel disconnected from them over the past couple of weeks and really needed to just be with them and talk to them. Josh was enjoying his summer and working like crazy to save up money. He had actually been spending quite a bit of time at Tyrone's house hanging out with him. He and Tracy were still full-speed ahead in his words. Sherita loved her children; their energy brought her great joy. As the night went on, dinner was good and Sherita knew she needed to get back to the house to sort out her friend's affairs.

"Thanks for dinner mom," Josh said.

"Always son," she replied.

The three headed home listening to Montell Jordan's "This Is How We do It," in full blast on the radio. Sherita felt good, she needed to laugh, and besides, she knew that whatever awaited her in that envelope was not going to make her happy. Sherita really wished she could have spoken with Allison. She felt sad at the thought of losing her friend.

Chapter 17

Dear Sherita –

If you are reading this letter, then by now I am in a state that will not allow me to communicate with you on my own. Let me start by saying I am so sorry for isolating myself from you these past few years. It has been a really scary time for me and I really just didn't know how to share with you or anyone else what I was experiencing. I know that is no excuse, so all I can hope is that you will forgive me.

Sherita, I love you so much. You have always been the sister I never had in my life. I appreciate all the love and support you showed me unconditionally even up to the bitter end. I know that you have probably been by my side since the moment you found out and for that, my friend, I am truly grateful. I asked Dr. Altman to contact you because you are the closest thing to family that I have and I knew that no matter what, you would make sure that everything was handled and taken care of appropriately.

I assume by now you have met little Miss Luckye. Isn't she adorable? She reminds me so much of you, Sherita, it is amazing. Her little sassy personality and comedic ways, she keeps me laughing. I named her Luckye because I was literally "lucky" to have made it through the pregnancy with her. She should feel as if she already knows you, because I talked about you all the time. Sherita, please make sure you remain a constant figure in her life. I know that her dad will do the best job he can with her, but I want to make sure that she has you there in some way to help guide her through the pitfalls that I won't be able to help her navigate. I already had a discussion with her dad about the constant role I want you to have in her life, if you are willing to do so. Of all the things that is the most important to me, because I know that you will help her to remember me.

Sher, I don't want to be kept on life support, so please give permission for the hospital to take me off the machines when the time comes. I know this is a hard thing to do, but please know that I am at peace with the decision and ready to claim my place in heaven (if God will have me). I have enclosed a list of about 15 people to contact once I pass to invite to a small memorial service. I want to be cremated and my ashes given to Luckye in an urn that you guys select together.

All of the documents for my life insurance are enclosed in this envelope and you will see where there are three $100,000 policies. The three of them have you listed as beneficiary so you shouldn't have any problems making the claims. The first, one please use to cover whatever additional costs are necessary for my services and remaining hospital bills, which shouldn't be any more than $25,000 total. The remaining $75,000 you can give to Charles for him and Luckye. The second one, I would like for you to put in an interest-bearing trust fund for Luckye to receive upon her 21st birthday. The last one Sher is all for you. I know you don't want it, but I have always told you that if I ever had money, I would take care of you; and here is my opportunity to do just that. I hope that you will use it to take a nice long vacation to an island and dance the night away in my honor. I know that I can "count on you," and that is why I chose you Sherita Coleman. I have pretty much taken care of everything, I don't have any outstanding bills, Charles has instructions on what to do with my personal affects and belongings and all other arrangements have been taken care of, I just need you to help execute. You are an amazing friend and person, Sherita, and I have been blessed to know you for my time here on this earth.

Please know that you will have a guardian angel in heaven looking out for you. Please give Tyrone and the kids my love.

I will see you in heaven,

Ally

P.S. Sing for me...

Chapter 18

Sherita carried out the wishes of her dying friend. The day of the memorial ceremony there was a calm presence in the air that somehow resonated Allison's spirit. Sherita was able to contact all of the people on the list, most of whom made it to the service and one-by-one expressed their deepest condolences for her loss. As Sherita sat on a back pew near the doorway of the chapel, she felt a hand touch her shoulder. Before she could turn to look, she felt Luckye lay her head against her shoulder with a single tear streaming down her face.

"Aunt Sher," she said softly.

"Thank you for being such an amazing friend to my mother, she loved you so much and she was very lucky to have you."

Now with tears in her eyes, Sherita was in amazement at the words coming from this 7-year-old little girl.

"No sweetie, I am the one who was lucky to have her," Sherita said as she winked her eye at Luckye.

"Aunt Sher, would it be OK if I came to visit you at your house sometimes?" Luckye asked.

"Absolutely!" Sherita proclaimed.

"You are welcome anytime you want to come. As a matter of fact, I will plan something fun for us to do in the next couple of months, and see if your Dad will let you come hang out for the weekend. "Deal?"

"That would be awesome!" Luckye smiled.

The two shared a strong hug of comfort and prepared to continue on with the rest of their lives. Sherita was glad that she would have an opportunity to be a part of Luckye's life. She knew that it would be a rewarding experience sharing with her how brilliant her mother was and how much she loved and cherished her.

After the memorial service, Sherita took a couple of days off before heading back to work to get her mind together. Josh and Alana were busy preparing for the rapidly approaching end of summer and were in and out the house periodically.

It was a rare occasion that Sherita had the entire house to herself and she decided to take full advantage of the opportunity. She opened the blinds in the room to allow the sun to shine in and turned on the radio to get her going. While milling around, the doorbell rang. Not expecting any guests, Sherita reluctantly went to the door. There was a flower delivery lady standing on the porch holding the most amazing display of tropical flowers she had ever seen.

"Yes?" she yelled through the door.

"I have a flower delivery for Ms. Sherita Coleman," the voice said.

Sherita opened the door, signed for the flowers and headed to the kitchen to see who they were from. The card read: *An amazing day should always start in an amazing way with an amazing bouquet for an amazing woman. Kroy.* Dumbfounded, Sherita stood with a smile on her face. She had completely forgotten about the gorgeous stranger who captured her attention in the hotel lobby during Nicole's bridal shower. She searched for her cellphone to give him a call, but then thought maybe she should call Kendra first. As the phone rang, she was nervous, not sure how to respond to such a great gesture.

"Hi sweetie, how are you feeling today?" asked Kendra.

Sherita looked at the phone, there was never a time that Kendra answered with such a calm demeanor, something must be wrong with her.

"Kendra, girl, you OK?" Sherita asked jokingly.

"What?" asked Kendra with a hint of frustration.

"I am trying to be more in touch with my softer side," she replied.

"Ok, softer side," Sherita joked and laughed out loud.

"Whatever, what are you up to this morning? I thought you were going to sleep in," asked Kendra.

"Well, that was my intent and then I decided to just get up and do some things around the house and the doorbell rang with a delivery."

"Delivery?" Kendra asked.

"Kendra, girl I am standing in my kitchen looking at the most beautiful display of tropical flowers you could ever imagine in life," explained Sherita.

"Ok, so who are they from?"

"Well, the card reads and I quote: 'An amazing day should always start in an amazing way with an amazing bouquet for an amazing woman'."

"Well, that's AMAZING!" "Now who the hell are they from?"

"Girl, they are from Kroy!"

"WHO!?"

"Girl, Kroy, the guy from the lobby at the hotel from Nicole's bridal shower," Sherita explained.

"OHHHHH the fine-as-hell brother with the accent," Kendra screamed.

"You know, I meant to ask you about him! How the hell did he get your

information?"

"Well, we did exchange numbers that day, but it has all been such a blur,

that I had honestly forgot all about the man," replied Sherita. "Not sure

how he got my home address though."

"Wait, wait, wait in the midst of ALL that was going on, you managed to

exchange phone numbers with the finest brother in the building and

yo'ass claim you don't remember him? Heffa, you crazy," proclaimed

Kendra.

"Girl, I am serious, I have not given him a second thought since that day.

Besides he doesn't even live in the United States," explained Sherita.

"Ok, so what are you going to do now?" Kendra asked. "What are you

going to tell Lamont about this enormous bouquet of flowers that it is

clear his ass ain't bought?"

Sherita hadn't thought about that.

"Shit, I don't know. Honestly, Lamont has been acting so strange lately;

he probably won't even be fazed by them. Besides, ever since he moved

back into his place, he really doesn't spend that much time over here anymore anyway." "Lately? Hmph, hell his ass has always been strange," Kendra interjected. "But I digress," she said.

"Ok, so what should I do about Kroy?" "Should I call him?"

"Sherita, girl, don't make me hang up on yo'ass – HELL YEAH you should call him and at least say thank you for the damn flowers," Kendra said.

"Ok, ok, ok…I will call him," Sherita said with a sigh.

"Uh, like NOW! Call me back!"

Sherita could hear what sounded like an instant dial tone from where Kendra had hung up on her. Now extremely nervous, she searched her purse for the napkin that Kroy wrote his number on that day. Not finding it right off, she was getting a bit concerned that she had accidentally thrown it in the trash over the past couple months or hell even blown her nose on it in the midst of all the crying. She took her time, kept looking and sure enough, she had managed to neatly fold it into a nice square and tucked it away at the back of her wallet with her emergency cash stash. She sat staring at the number for a few minutes and rehearsed in her head what she would say. While dialing the number, she could feel butterflies in her stomach. The phone rang for what seemed like five minutes.

Sherita was feeling somewhat relieved, thinking this way she could leave a nice voicemail message and be done. Just as she was preparing her message he answered.

"Good day, how may I help you?" the deep island-tone voice asked.

"Um, yes – may I speak with Kroy LaBeouf, please?" Sherita asked.

"Speaking, who's on the line?" he asked.

"Um, hi Kroy it is Sherita," she said taking a deep breath.

"Ahhh…the amazing woman, how are you Mi'Amore?"

"I am good, thank you – I received the beautiful or shall I say AMAZING bouquet of flowers this morning and it really made me smile," she said.

"Well, that was my intent. Mission accomplished," he said jokingly.

"I can't believe you sent me flowers, that was so thoughtful of you, thank you," she continued.

"Well, after I did not hear from you while I was in town, I figured something had gone wrong with your family member, and I wanted to give you the space you needed to handle whatever you were going through. I have been praying for you and your family and figured it has been the better part of a month or so since we met and perhaps some flowers would make you smile," he explained.

Blushing, Sherita nodded in agreement.

"Well you did just that," she assured him.

"So, are you here in Atlanta? How did you get my address?"

"Well, I am not in Atlanta, I am at home in Trinidad and I called to the office number you provided and mentioned that I wanted to send some flowers to your home and your assistant gave me the information," he explained.

"Hmmm, I may need to have a discussion with my assistant. She has been extremely free-flowing with my personal information here lately," Sherita said laughing.

"I apologize, I don't want to get her in trouble," said Kroy.

"No, no – I am just kidding, I am glad she gave it to you. The flowers are really beautiful and fast becoming my favorites every time I turn to look at them." "Well, they were handpicked by me here in Trinidad yesterday with specific instructions on when they needed to be sent via FedEx to ensure that they were fresh upon arrival. I am glad you like them," he said.

"So, when do you plan to come back to Atlanta? I feel as if I at least owe you lunch or dinner or something for your kind gesture," she inquired.

"Well, it will not be for a couple more months before I make it back to Atlanta, but you are most certainly welcome to come visit me here in Trinidad," he suggested. Sherita's eyes extended to the size of a half dollar wondering if she had heard him correctly.

"Wow, that is sweet! But I couldn't impose upon you in that manner. Thank you for the offer, though," she said nicely.

"Sweet? I am not trying to be 'sweet' Mi'Amore; I would love for you to consider a visit to the island. Have you ever been?"

"No, I have never been to Trinidad, I am sure it is beautiful."

"It is paradise," he replied. "I tell you what, give it some thought. My family is having our annual celebration in a couple of weeks for the summer carnival season, you can come down and be a part of the festivities," he insisted.

"Wow, that sounds like fun!" Sherita replied.

"How 'bout this? I will message you with the information later today, and you can decide by the end of the week. If you agree, I will make the arrangements. Deal?" "Sure," she said.

"Great."

"Thank you again for the call Sherita, I look forward to chatting with you again soon and hopefully seeing you in a few weeks," he said.

"Thank you Kroy, for the flowers, we will be in touch," she said as she hung up the phone.

Completely overwhelmed by the conversation, Sherita couldn't believe she was actually intrigued by the thought of spending some time in Trinidad. Just as she went to dial the phone to call Kendra, she had already beaten her to the punch. "Hello," Kendra said on the other end.

"Girl, I was just dialing the phone to call you," Sherita said.

"Yeah, yeah, yeah – OK so what he say?" Kendra asked with excitement.

"Well…..," Sherita said with lingering intensity.

"Heffa! Well…nothing! What did the man say? Did you talk to him?" yelled Kendra.

"Yes, Kendra I spoke with him and he is jaw-dropping."

"We could see that Sher. Now what the hell did the man say? Did you tell him you got the flowers?"

"Ok, so I told him thank you for the flowers and he mentioned that he had hand-picked them specifically for me yesterday and had them sent overnight via FedEx to ensure a timely and 'fresh' arrival," she said adoringly.

"Girl, that is some shit!"

"Kendra, he asked me to come to Trinidad in two weeks for the summer carnival celebration."

"And I hope you said yes," Kendra replied.

"Come on Kendra, now you know I can't just up and go to Trinidad with some man I met in a hotel and not have some sort of explanation for Lamont," she insisted.

"Why the hell you can't? Last I checked, Lamont, no longer lives with you…you don't live with him. And besides didn't you just say that ever since the two of you broke up and he moved back to his place he really hadn't been spending much time over there anymore? So, unless you all have made some vows that I am not aware of, y'all aint married to each other and therefore Lamont is not a factor in this equation. And besides, you said it yourself Sher, Lamont has been acting a little strange lately. And hell, you could use a break for a minute," Kendra said convincingly.

"Yeah, I know. I told him I would think about it."

"What are you thinking about Sher?"

"I don't know, I am just thinking," she said confusingly.

"Girl, let me meet a man that look that damn good, from another country, send my ass some flowers OVERNIGHT ON FEDEX and he invite me to come to visit in 80-degree weather with white-sand beaches. Hmph, trust me, I would be stretched out on a lounge chair with an umbrella in my drink on the beach listening to "Caribbean Queen" by Billy Ocean so quick, fast, and in a hurry, baby he would think I had signed up to vote in his damn country," Kendra said assuredly. "Kendra, I will think about it," Sherita said annoyingly.

"I'm just saying."

"Alright girl, I hear you. Let me get some clothes on, I will call you later," Sherita said.

"Ok Sher, enjoy your day off."

Sherita hung up the phone and sat down at the kitchen table gazing at the beautiful display of flowers on the table. She had to admit, she could use a nice long getaway. Maybe it would be fun? Perhaps doing something wild and crazy like flying halfway across the country to visit a man she'd only met once was just what she needed to get back in gear. The past few months had been tough and she could use a little rest and relaxation on a nice quiet beach. Hmmm.

Chapter 19

Lamont sat nervously in the waiting room of his lawyer's office anxiously looking at his watch every few seconds. He could not believe he had allowed this to go on for so long and could now possibly be facing jail time for the destructive behavior of his business partner. The nerve of Chris, to go and get them both mixed up in a money-laundering scheme and leave Lamont clueless about the whole situation. Lamont knew he shouldn't have gotten mixed up with Chris again. Ever since they were kids, it seemed as though trouble followed this dude and somehow Lamont managed to always be right in the middle of it. Just when he thought his life was on track, things took an awful turn for the worse. He just couldn't see himself going back to jail. The past few months have been taxing and not being able to share this information with Sherita was eating him up inside. He could only imagine what she would think of him. Things were already rocky between the two of them and something like this would surely send her over the edge.

"Mr. Washington, Attorney Jones will see you now," said the receptionist at the front desk.

Lamont stood and took a deep breath as he buttoned the jacket to his suit.

"Lamont, good to see you," said Mr. Jones as he reached to shake hands.

"Please, have a seat. Can I get you some coffee or some water?"

"No, thank you, I just want my life back," Lamont replied.

"Well, it seems as though you have gotten yourself into a bit of a quandary with the recent activities from your organization. Why don't you start at the top and tell me what happened."

"My partner Chris and I started our organization about five years ago. As with most start-ups, we both invested quite a bit of our own money to help keep things afloat until we were able to make the necessary connections here in the city to help secure investors and key contributors. He ultimately handled the majority of the in-take of the funds and I pretty much went out to make the pitch and secure the deals. We put the majority of the funds back into the community and the youth we serviced, providing tutoring, scholarship opportunities and other key programming initiatives. Our largest funder came when I was able to secure a three-year deal at $250,000 a year from The Wagner Group. In the contract, we were suppose to create supplemental programming to coincide with what we currently offered in the community. The caveat is that they gave us the funds up-front with the expectation that we would

report back quarterly with how the money was being spent. Again, that

whole aspect of the business, I was under the impression that Chris had it

under control. He was making sure our staff was paid, our expenses

were covered and that the monies were allocated accordingly. Or so I

thought. Because these were federal funds, we started getting letters in

the mail from the government regarding the money and all of a sudden

there wasn't anything in our operating account. I still, to this day, don't

have a full clue as to what happened and now my name is on the line and

I am facing jail time for what appears to be a money-laundering scheme.

And to top it all off, and make matters even worse, The Wagner Group is

where my girlfriend works. She was initially the person I met with when

I made the proposal for our organization. Although she had nothing to

do with the acceptance process, I still haven't told her anything about all

of what has happened. I am afraid that once it all comes out that she will

inadvertently be involved through no fault of her own. Mr. Jones, I just

don't know what to do." "Hmm, yeah, I would say you are in a bit of a

mess Mr. Washington," replied Attorney Jones.

"Well, let me ask you this, why haven't you mentioned any of this to your girlfriend?"

"Look, Sherita and I started dating shortly after we landed the deal. We immediately agreed that we wouldn't mix business with pleasure and that way she wouldn't be in any type of conflict-of-interest situation with her job. So, we don't discuss work. She and I have been together for almost a year and up until a few months ago, when all of this stuff started happening, we were very happy. However, with me trying to figure this shit out and get everything back on track it has been difficult. I moved back into my place some weeks ago, she and I were having arguments about the craziest stuff and on top of that she has had a rough couple of months herself with the death of her friend. Seriously, this shit is ruining my life and I am afraid that the worst is still yet to come," Lamont said with despair.

"Well, money laundering is a very serious offense Mr. Washington, and in many instances can carry anywhere between 5 to 10 plus years in federal prison. And given your previous criminal record, I don't know that this is going to be an open-and-shut case for you. Honestly, by all accounts it looks like you and your partner both could be facing a significant amount of jail time. Now, I see here that your court date is scheduled for one month from today on September 1. We have a lot of work to do between now and then. I suggest you find the courage to share this information with your girlfriend Mr. Washington. She deserves that much from you. Otherwise she is going to find out from another source and make matters worse." Lamont sat for a moment massaging his temples. He knew that what Mr. Jones was saying was correct; he just didn't want to break Sherita's heart. How could he convince her that he had nothing to do with this crazy-ass scam and at the same time hope that she would understand and somehow forgive him?

"Look, Mr. Washington, I will schedule a meeting with the District Attorney to see if there is any type of deal that can be worked out to avoid extensive jail time. But I can't make any promises."

"Thank you Mr. Jones," he said while standing to leave. As Lamont waited for the elevator, his phone started ringing. It was Josh calling.

"Hey Josh what's up?"

"Hey Lamont, uhm, I just got home and thought I better call you and let you know that a couple of federal agents stopped by the house looking for you about 20 minutes ago. Not sure what they wanted, but they left a card and I told them that you no longer lived here, but that if I saw you I would pass along the information. Dude, is everything OK? Are you in some sort of trouble?"

"What? Is your mom at home?" Lamont asked immediately.

"Naw man, it's just me. Are you alright?" Josh was concerned.

"Yea, yea I am fine. Thanks Josh for calling me. Please don't say anything to your mother. I don't want to worry her. I will take care of it."

"Ok," Josh replied. "But hey Lamont, whatever you got going on, don't put my mom in the middle of it," he said sternly and hung up the phone.

Chapter 20

Alana felt like she was running out of time. She had less than 24 hours to finish up all the running around she needed to do before she would head off to school. She decided to stop by the mall to look for a nice winter coat to take so she wouldn't have to figure that out once she got to New York. It had truly been a long and busy summer and she was looking forward to the idea of a little retail therapy. Browsing about the store, she noticed the back of a young woman who resembled her friend Janet. Alana and Janet hadn't spoken in quite some time and she thought it would be nice to see her friend. Janet's attitude toward Alana changed over the course of time once Alana and Delton became an item. Janet felt like Alana intentionally went out with Delton to keep him from liking her in the first place. Alana tried unsuccessfully on several occasions to explain to Janet that Delton never had an interest in her and that she would never intentionally go after a guy that a friend has her sights set on. The two ended their friendship and barely acknowledged one another whenever they were within vicinity. Alana always felt it was just stupid to break up a friendship over a guy. As Alana got closer, she realized it was Janet and decided to let bygones be bygones and approach her to say hello.

"Janet?" Alana said as she approached her friend. "I thought that was you, how are you?"

Somewhat caught off guard, Janet turned around at the sound of Alana's voice. "What are you doing here?" she asked with an attitude.

"Uhm, hello, shopping, it is the mall," Alana shot back sarcastically.

Realizing this encounter was not going to go the way she envisioned it, Alana decided to just let it go.

"Listen," she said as she threw her hands in the air to symbolize a truce. "I didn't approach you to start no beef with you Janet. I just thought I would put our differences aside and say hello. My bad."

"Well maybe you should have just pretended as if you didn't see me," said Janet in a nasty tone.

Rolling her eyes and becoming irritated, Alana decided this was a bad idea and turned to walk away.

"Ok Janet, have a nice life."

"Oh trust me sweetie, I intend to have a fabulous life, Alana, as Mrs. Delton Jemison and raising our child."

Unsure if what she had just heard was correct, Alana turned to face her friend who at this point was in full view and visibly pregnant. The thought hadn't crossed Alana's mind that the entire conversation was taking place in the middle of the baby layette section of the department store.

"What?"

"That's right Lan, Delton and I are married and expecting a baby the first of the year," she said flashing her ring finger and a sly smile on her face. Speechless, Alana all of a sudden felt nauseated.

"Well congratulations, to the end of your life," Alana snarled.

As she turned around to leave again, there stood Delton in shock. Holding back tears, Alana didn't have words to speak. She gave him a look of disgust as she pushed past him to head for the escalator.

"Lan, I'm sorry," he shouted after her. It was too late she had disappeared down the escalator headed toward the parking lot.

Breathing in a hyperventilating state, Alana managed to get the key out to open the car door. She sat in the car in complete shock. Unsure of the feelings she was experiencing, she was more so angry with herself for even having a reaction. After all, she and Delton were done and he was free to be with whomever he wanted. Alana just wasn't prepared for it to be Janet. While she sat in the car contemplating if whether or not she should go back in the mall, her cellphone started to ring. It was Josh.

"Hello," she answered solemnly.

"Lan, where are you?" Josh asked intently.

"What Josh? I am so not in the mood right now."

"Seriously Lan, I need you to come home before mom gets here. It is important," he said.

Hearing a sense of urgency in her brother's voice, Alana turned her attention to him.

"Josh, what's going on? Are you OK?"

"Yes. I am fine, but I need to talk to you, before mom gets home."

"I will be there shortly."

As Alana headed home, she couldn't help but replay the events from the mall over and over again in her head. She never in a million years would have imagined this turn of events taking place.

Pulling into the driveway, she could see Josh sitting on the front porch with a look of uncertainty on his face. Alana sat down on the step next to her brother. Josh reached over and handed his sister the card that the federal agent had left with him earlier. Looking at the card, Alana's eyes got big. "Josh, what did you do?" she asked her brother.

Leaning over and snatching the card from his sister's hand he says, "I didn't do anything, but your boy Lamont, he is up to something."

"Huh," Alana asked with intrigue.

"What is going on?"

"When I got home from the park a little bit ago, two guys in this cop car pulled up in the driveway. They asked me if I knew Lamont Washington and how or where to find him. I told them, yeah, I knew him, but that he didn't live here anymore and I didn't know where he had gone. The guy gave me this look like he thought I was lying and handed me this card and said, to have Lamont get in contact with them if I see him. I said aight and headed in the house," he said.

Sitting with her hand over her mouth, Alana was completely in shock.

"So, what'd you do, did you call Mom?"

"No, I called Lamont."

"Shut-up! What'd he say?" she asked feverishly.

"I told him that these dudes was looking for him and wanted him to call em'. I asked him if he was in some sort of trouble and he just said he would take care of it. He asked me not to tell Mom and I said OK, but warned him not to put Mom in the middle of it and I hung up."

"Josh! We have to tell Mom. What if she is in some sort of danger and doesn't know it based on whatever it is that Lamont has going on?"

"Well, here's the deal. We will be leaving tomorrow to drive you to school, so we will be gone for a few days. Hopefully, whatever is going on Lamont can get it together before we get back. Besides, Mom leaves Tuesday for her trip to Trinidad. I don't want to ruin it for her with something that may end up being nothing. Let's just play it by ear," Josh said.

"I don't know Josh, are you sure?"

"Yeah, let's just see what happens. Those guys didn't have any interest in Mom; they were specifically looking for Lamont. Besides, I'll give dad a heads up at some point this weekend so we will be prepared for whatever. Don't worry Lan, everything will be fine," he assured his sister.

Josh put his arm around his sister's shoulder and pulled her close to him for a hug. "So, what's going on with you? Did you find a coat?" he asked.

Looking off at the birds playfully chasing one another in the street, Alana was reminded about the uncomfortable encounter she had earlier at the mall.

"Delton and Janet got married and they are expecting a baby," she said with a long sigh.

"Wait a minute, do what?" he said in shock.

"You heard me," she reconfirmed. "That's what I got at the mall."

As Alana stood to go inside the house, Sherita pulled up in the driveway waving excitedly out the car window. Smiling from ear-to-ear this was the happiest the kids had seen Sherita in months. With a hand full of bags, it was apparent that she had been shopping. Alana and Josh decided to let their mother have her moment and keep the events of the day to themselves. Josh went to grab the bags from his mother's hands and embraced her with a loving hug and kiss on the forehead. Alana watched silently as her mother danced up the sidewalk modeling what appeared to be a Caribbean inspired scarf that she had purchased for her trip. "Alana sweetie, guess what! I bought you a coat!" she announced excitedly. Wow, that was just what Alana wanted to hear.

Chapter 21

Sherita anxiously anticipated landing in Trinidad. As she patiently flipped back through the People magazine she had reviewed several times, she honestly couldn't believe she was doing this. She was truly stepping outside her comfort zone by agreeing to visit a complete stranger who lived halfway across the globe. There had been a lot going on with her the past few months and she was looking forward to a relaxing vacation. As the pilot's voice came across the loud speaker giving instruction for the flight attendant's to prepare the cabin for arrival, Sherita leaned back and closed her eyes to pray silently.

"Lord, I thank you for the many opportunities and surprises you continue to bestow upon my life. Please let this trip be one of meaning and fun and filled with the spirit of You. Thank you Lord for my family's safe travel to and from New York to drop off my precious Alana and I pray, Lord, that you keep her safe in Your arms at all times. I pray, Lord, that you watch over my beautiful baby Josh and just make sure that Your will is done in all of our lives at all times Lord. Thank you, Amen."

Sherita's random prayer was all over the place, but she felt like if nothing else, God got the gist of what she was saying. It was late in the evening, nearing midnight. Kroy had called prior to the flight to wish Sherita safe

travels and confirm that he would be waiting for her at the airport upon

her arrival. As she exited the plane, she was excited to see the sign that

read Bienvenido A Trinidad & Tobago. "*Welcome to Trinidad,*" she

whispered to herself with a smile and followed the signs toward customs.

Once her passport was stamped, it was official, she was in Trinidad.

Making her way through the baggage claim line Sherita was trying not to

look so displaced. Once she got her bags, she followed the instructions

Kroy had given her and headed down the escalator just to the left toward

the green parking deck sign. As she neared the bottom of the escalator

she could see Kroy standing at the base with another fabulous array of

flowers and a warm welcoming smile. The two embraced in a loving

hug that would have given a stranger the impression that they had been

together for most of their life. Sherita instantly felt comfortable with

Kroy as he reached down to grab her luggage. "Mi'Amore, I am so

happy to see you," he said in his seductively accented voice. "Do you

always speak in poetic innuendos," she asked with a smile.

"Only when the muse before me provides feelings of emotional joy," he

replied. The late night travel out of the country was taking a toll on

Sherita; it was way past her bedtime. Too excited to sleep, she needed to stay alert to make sure she didn't miss a moment of this seemingly magical week that was in store.

Kroy had completely taken care of all of the arrangements. All Sherita had to do was say yes and in less than 24 hours she had a roundtrip first-class ticket delivered via FedEx. She insisted on at least covering the cost of her hotel stay, but Kroy was not having it, making sure she understood that she would spend the week with him and his family at their estate.

As they pulled up to the massive wrought iron gate, Sherita could see a palatial mansion certainly fit for a king. Overwhelmed by the innate beauty of it at night, she could only imagine what to expect come daylight. Kroy came around to open the door for Sherita before getting the bags out the back of the truck. As she stood waiting, the quiet calm in the air was so refreshing. She took a minute to take in the unique sounds of the night, welcoming the light chirps of the nearby crickets, enjoying the aroma of the surrounding flowers and imagining the view that was gently illuminated by the light from the fullness of the moon. "Kroy, this is amazing," she said.

"This is just the beginning, Mi'Amore."

The house was still, as all had settled in for the night. Kroy escorted Sherita to her room, just down the hall from him. As she settled into the space, he sat admiringly in a chair watching her with a smile.

"Why are you looking at me like that?" she whispered.

"I just think you're beautiful," he said softly.

Sitting down on the bed, she was exhausted but managed to say thank you. As he stood to leave, he says "OK, I am going to let you get some sleep and I will see you in the morning. Or should I say shortly," he chuckled. Reaching down, he grabbed her hands and gently kissed them both.

"Goodnight," she replied, and he disappeared down the hall.

Glancing at the clock it was now 2:00 a.m. and even though it was late, she wouldn't hear the end of it if she didn't at least call Kendra to tell her she had arrived.

"Hell, I was just about to call Jessie Jackson to come rescue you. Why are you just now calling me?" Kendra said with an air of frustration in her voice.

"Girl, I just got here literally about 15 minutes ago. The flight was four hours long and then it took another hour or so to get through customs and baggage claim. So, by the time I made it through the line Kroy was there waiting for me and I didn't want to be rude and talk on the phone. I am sorry, I am fine," she insisted.

"Ok, good. I was about to think maybe it wasn't such a good idea to send you off. So, how is it so far? How does he look?" Kendra asked deviantly.

"Kendra, girl, he still looks the same. So far I am tired as hell and about to go to sleep. I will call you in the morning and give you the run down," Sherita said. "Alright, alright…as long as you are good, I guess I can wait until daybreak," Kendra said laughing with a sigh.

"Thanks girl."

"Sher, please have a good time. You deserve to just let loose and live in the moment."

"I will. Love you."

"Love you, too."

Hmm, let loose and live in the moment. Sherita thought about the words her friend spoke in the phone and thought to herself that is exactly what she intended to do. She laid down and fell asleep instantly. Sherita woke the next morning to dancing sunlight on the bedroom wall, birds singing and a sweet aroma mixed with fresh tropical flowers from outside and what appeared to be breakfast cooking in the kitchen. As she slowly cracked open the door to her room, she saw she had a clean break for the bathroom before she encountered anyone in the house.

"Good morning, beautiful. Did you sleep well?" asked the soft voice of a woman. Turning to respond, Sherita was greeted by the warm embrace of Mrs. Auhna LaBeauf, Kroy's mom.

"Oh, good morning, Ma'am," she said shyly with a smile. "Yes, thank you. It was the best rest I have had in weeks." Sherita sighed.

"Well, good. After you get cleaned up, please join us for breakfast in the family room," Auhna insisted.

"Yes, Ma'am. I will be right there."

Sherita quickly pulled herself together. She ran her fingers through her hair, washed her face, and brushed her teeth. She figured she would jump in the shower after breakfast and not keep the family waiting. Walking through the house, she admired the many family photos and wonderful works of art. As she gazed at the many pictures of Kroy, she couldn't help but shake her head at the gorgeous specimen of a man he was. His humbleness made him even more attractive. "GOOD MORNING Mi'Amore!" Kroy said with a huge smile as he stood to greet Sherita in the family room.

Smiling, she was a bit shy, but felt right at home. Kroy was the youngest of four children and the only boy in the family. That much was evident based upon the pictures and trophies of his childhood accomplishments as what appeared to be a little league soccer player.

"Good morning," Sherita said with a smile back as she accepted the empty seat at the end of the table.

Kroy introduced Sherita to his mother once again, two of his sisters and his niece. They were all such beautiful people; Sherita was in awe of their presence.

"Ms. Sherita darling, I have made an array of treats for you this morning, so please don't be shy," said Auhna in her very heavy Trinidadian accent.

"Thank you. I appreciate all of this. This place is amazing. It's like paradise," she said.

Smiling with pleasure, Auhna shook her head in agreement and lightly touched Sherita on the shoulder to provide a sense of comfort. As breakfast came to an end, everyone was off to their normal way of life in this paradise environment. Kroy had plans to show Sherita around town while running a few errands. He was excited to have her here. They had made it a point to speak by phone at least twice a day over the past few weeks and had become quite comfortable with one another.

"Ok, Mr. LaBeauf! Now that you have me here, we can continue our conversation about life," Sherita said while riding shotgun.

"Well, as I mentioned on the phone, my family owns and operates one of the oldest and largest international art galleries in the world. For as far back as I can remember, we have always dealt with unique art, artifacts and historic memoirs. My great-grandfather started the business in the earlier 1900s in a small town in Trinidad called Arima. That is where my parents grew-up, and were married. My great-grandfather passed it on to his son and then my grandfather passed on to my father, who has now been in charge for more than 30 years. We all work in the family business in some aspect or another. I am the Chief Operating Officer and spend much of my time traveling back and forth to the United States working out deals with buyers and sellers in the industry," Kroy said

with pride in his family. "Wow! That is amazing. I love that you all

still keep the business alive and successful after all these years," she said.

"Well, we have to, if we want to eat," he said with a light chuckle.

"So, have you lived in Trinidad all of your life?"

"No, I lived in New York for 10 years and attended the University."

Laughing out loud, Sherita said, "the University huh? That sounds like

some 'Coming to America'- type stuff."

Gazing at her lovingly, he joined in the laughter.

"Yeah, not quite that, but I spent a semester at NYU."

"Oh wow, how cool is that! My daughter Alana is in her first semester at

NYU. Her dad and her brother just took her to school last week," Sherita

said. "That is great! She will love it. It is a great learning institution and

New York has a lot to offer and see. I try to go back two or three times a

year to visit friends." He said. "So, have you ever been married? I mean,

I know you have the one son, but I don't think we discussed how he got

here?" Sherita asked inquisitively.

"Yes. I was married for 7 years. She was my high-school sweetheart.

We were both very young and dumb and didn't know how to be parents let alone be married at such an early age. But, you know how that goes, especially when you think you know it all."

"Tell me about it," Sherita said in agreement reflecting briefly on her marriage to Tyrone.

"But, we have been divorced for going on 10 years now and we have a healthy relationship that allows us to raise our son together. She has remarried and has two additional children, so things are good," he added.

"Hmph, sounds like me and my ex-husband. We do a great job parenting our kids together. He just recently remarried as well," she shared.

"Good. Good to know."

"So, do you think you will ever get remarried?" she asked coyly.

"Oh, I hope. And soon," he said with certainty.

"What about you? Are you open to re-marrying?" Kroy asked.

"Well, I would like to one day," Sherita said.

"I just recently ended a nearly year-long relationship and right now, I am just going with the flow. Love is always a possibility," she said.

"Hmmm, I see. I didn't realize you had just ended a recent relationship," he said. "Yeah, we broke up a few months ago. Things just weren't going the way I or I guess it is safe to say "we" envisioned them and so we both decided to call it quits. He had a lot going on and I just didn't

have the strength to deal with the drama," Sherita shared.

Chapter 22

Josh and Tyrone were on their way back to Atlanta from dropping Alana

off at school. Her first night in the dorm was weird and she spent most

of the night unpacking her stuff. For some reason, her roommate hadn't

arrived yet and that gave Alana the advantage of making the first

selection of what side of the room she wanted. Glancing at the clock, she

saw that it was getting late and she needed to be up early in the morning

to be in line at financial aid. As she lay staring at the ceiling, Alana was

very excited about being in New York, but, she also already missed her

family. This would certainly take some getting use to. Maneuvering her

way through the crowded streets in New York City, Alana was

desperately attempting to blend in while at the same time trying to figure

out where she was going. As she approached the building to the

administration and financial aid office, she was relieved. Once inside,

she noticed a line of about 15 other students some standing, some sitting

and all looking uniquely artsy. She secured her place in line and

searched her bag for a magazine to peruse as she waited.

"Hello."

Alana was suddenly distracted by the high-pitched voice of the young lady in front of her.

"Hi," she replied.

"Are you a new student?" inquired the young lady.

"Yes, I am a freshman," Alana said.

Completely facing Alana at this point, the young lady extended her hand in introduction.

"I'm Bella," she said.

Complying with the handshake, she replied "Alana."

"Nice to meet you, Alana. I am a freshman as well and was hoping to meet someone soon," Bella said with a nervous chuckle. "Are you from New York?"

"I know, right. No, I am not from New York, I am from Atlanta. How bout you?" asked Alana.

"Wow, Atlanta! I love Georgia. I have family that lives down there. I am from California," Bella replied.

As the two continued with their awkward exchange of pleasantries, the line slowly started to move.

"Excuse me, is this the line for financial aid," asked the young man who walked up behind Alana?

Bella shook her head yes and Alana replied "yes."

A few minutes went by and finally another introduction took place.

"Are you ladies freshmen?" he asked.

"Yes," they said in unison.

"My name is Nehemiah," said the young man.

"Hi, Nehemiah, I am Alana and this is Bella."

As the line started moving, the three all shared the same sentiments of being excited about attending NYU.

"Where are you from Nehemiah?" asked Bella.

"Charlotte, North Carolina," he said with a southern drawl.

"Cool, I am from Atlanta," chimed in Alana.

"Cali," offered up Bella with a peace symbol thrown in the air.

"Nice," he said.

"So, listen, I was thinking about grabbing some pizza after this stuff is taken care of, would you ladies like to join me?" Nehemiah asked.

The two girls looked at one another for assurance from the other and simultaneously shrugged their shoulders in agreement.

"Great, sounds like a date," he said with a smile.

"Ok, guys I know this is going to sound corny, but can we all take a picture and create a lasting memory? I am big on photos and I want to remember what we were like the first day we met for years to come. Is that OK?" asked Alana feverishly.

"Long as we each get a copy!" replied Bella.

"Yeah, I want one, too," chimed Nehemiah.

As Alana solicited the help of a nearby stranger to take a photo of she and her new friends, they all were reeling with excitement. New York was already turning out to be amazing. Although she missed her family, she knew that she would make them proud no matter what.

"Ok everyone, smile," said the stranger.

And just like that, with the click of a button and a flash that lit the way to the future, the three would be inseparable from this day forward.

Josh laid across the bed talking to Tracy on the phone while tossing a tennis-ball in the air. As much as he hated to admit it, he really missed Alana. Not having her around every day was going to be more of an adjustment than he anticipated. "Hello," Tracy said in an annoyed tone.

"Huh? Oh, yeah I'm sorry sweetie, I was in another world for a minute," he said. "Ahh seems like you have been a little distant for the past couple of days. Josh, is everything OK? Tell me what is going on," Tracy insisted.

"Yo, I am good sweetheart. Just somewhat missing my Mom and my sister I guess."

"What? You, miss your sister! I didn't think I would ever hear you admit to that," she said laughing out loud.

"I know right. Hey and don't you ever tell her I said that or else I will deny it," he joked back. "No seriously, I do miss having Lan around to harass. She and I have been together forever and, it's just going to be weird not having her here to keep me straight."

"I am sure she misses you too, Josh. So, when does your mom get back from Trinidad?" she asked.

"Two more days, and I can't wait," he said with an unusual sigh. Things had been kind of weird since the visit from the federal officers at the house a few days earlier. He hadn't heard from Lamont and still hadn't shared the information with his Dad. Although Josh was staying with Tyrone and Nicole while Sherita was out of town, he still went to the house every day to collect the mail and check on things. A couple of times he has seen some guys sitting in cars parked up the street. Josh felt like he should have at least mentioned it to his Mom about the visit by the two cops, but he really didn't want her to worry. She and Lamont had endured a pretty uncomfortable break-up and she was still dealing with the death of Aunt Ally and Lan's move to New York. It had gotten to the point that the only time he saw his mother smile was when she talked about her trip. Josh didn't want to destroy that for her, but he knew he needed to tell his dad and soon.

"Josh, get dressed and come go grab a bite with me," Tyrone half-knocked on the door and stuck his head in to get his son's attention.

"Yeah, OK Dad. I will be right out."

"Yo sweetheart, my dad wants me to go eat with him. I will give you a call when I get back if it isn't too late," he said to Tracy.

"Ok J. Hey, talk to your dad and get whatever is on your mind out into the open. I promise you will feel better," she said with comfort.

"Thanks Tracy, I will."

Josh and Tyrone arrived at their favorite soul food restaurant on Cascade Road. Once they placed their orders, the two made small talk about the varying characters of individuals that made up the environment in the room. Josh really loved and respected his mom and dad. He knew that his dad would provide the best advice in how to handle this situation with Lamont.

"Dad, I need to talk to you about something," Josh said with nervousness in his voice.

"Yeah son, what's on your mind?"

"Well, Dad, I think Lamont is in some sort of trouble. I don't quite know what it is, but last week a couple of federal agents showed up at the house looking for him and asking a bunch of questions."

"Go on," Tyrone said with intense anticipation in his voice as he wiped his mouth with his napkin.

"Well, I am sure you know that Mom and Lamont broke up a couple of months ago. Honestly, I think they had broken up longer than that, but were just going through the motions until Lamont finally moved out. Dad, I don't think Mom knows that Lamont is this trouble and I didn't mention it to her about the federal agents coming by the house," Josh said with a feeling of weights being lifted off of his shoulders.

"So, what did you do, son?"

"Well, I told the guys that Lamont didn't live there and that I hadn't seen him in weeks. They gave me a card and told me to tell him to call them if I see him. I took the card and after they were gone, I went in the house and called Lamont. I told him what had happened and asked him what was going on? He assured me that he would handle it and asked me not to tell Mom. I reluctantly agreed, but made it very clear to him that he needed to make sure that Mom wasn't going to be blindsided by something she wasn't aware of. He said OK and hung up."

Letting out a long sigh, Tyrone had a million questions running through his head. He was becoming increasingly angry with Lamont for putting his ex-wife and kids in a situation that they knew nothing about.

"Son, you know that it is your responsibility to always look out for the well-being of your mom and your sister. Nobody and I do mean NOBODY should ever come between you and your responsibility to the two of them. Now, I understand you did what you felt was the right thing to do by agreeing to not mention this to your mother, but son she is going to have to be brought in the loop. What if Lamont is involved in something that presents a situation that will bring harm to your mom unexpectedly, then what? So, as soon as she returns, we will need to tell her about the visit from the feds. It was wrong of Lamont to involve you in that manner and put you in a position to have to keep secrets from your Mom, but hopefully now, you know better. Going forward, do not ever let something like this happen again. Who else knows about this?" asked Tyrone.

"Just Lan," Josh said in shame with his head held down.

He knew he should've told his mom, but he really didn't want to hurt her and wanted her to just be happy.

"Ok son. We will take care of this in a couple of days when your mom returns. But son, next time don't wait, you come to us and tell us immediately. We can't help after the fact of something going wrong. You hear me," said Tyrone in a stern, yet caring voice.

"Yeah dad, I hear you. It won't happen again."

Just as Tyrone and Josh were finishing up dinner, Josh could hear his cellphone ringing. It was a number he didn't recognize.

"Hello?"

"What's up big-head, you miss me?" Alana said with excitement.

"Lan?" he asked, not fully recognizing his sister's voice.

"Duh, I haven't been gone that long silly that you don't recognize my voice, Josh," Alana said playfully.

"Girl, I didn't recognize the number so I wasn't sure who this was. You lucky I answered. You know I get stalked by crazy people ALL the time," he said in a joking tone.

Josh was relieved to hear his sister's voice. He missed her.

"So, what are you up to? Where you at? What's all that noise in the background?" she asked.

"Yo, slow your roll Sherlock, you asking like a million questions at a time. All up in my Kool-Aid shawty. If you must know, I am finishing up dinner with dad," he said sarcastically.

"Wow- dad? Wait, Josh did you tell him about Lamont," Alana was all of a sudden concerned for her brother.

"Yes, Lan. He knows about Lamont."

"Oh my God, what did he say? Is he angry with us for not telling Mom? Are you OK?" she inquired.

"I am fine Lan. Dad is good and we are going to tell Mom when she gets back from out of town in a couple of days. Everything will be OK," he assured her. "Would you like to speak with dad?"

"Ahh...yeah, sure," she said hesitantly.

Josh was awful calm for him having just told Dad what he told her just days earlier. She was almost hesitant to speak with Tyrone, because he would surely chastise her for any involvement she had in Josh's silence. Handing the phone to Tyrone, Josh motioned to let his dad know he was going to the restroom and would be right back.

"Hello, is this my little college angel?" Tyrone said lovingly.

"Hey Daddy. What are you doing?" Alana said in an excited tone.

"Hey baby-girl, how are you? I miss you so much. How are you adjusting in the Big Apple?"

"Oh wow, Daddy it is amazing. I am so excited about being here. I have made two good friends already and I am just really in a happy place," she said smiling. "Ahhh, that is great honey, I am glad to hear things are going well. What about your classes?"

"We start on Monday. I was able to get most of the classes I wanted with the exception of one, but I will be able to take it next semester. I also managed to get everything done in financial aid that you told me to take care of the other day. You should get the information in the mail soon."

"Perfect, I am very proud of you sweetheart," he said.

"Thank you, Daddy."

"Lan, I do want to say that I am a little disappointed in how you and your brother have handled this situation with Lamont. Under no circumstances should you guys ever keep anything so serious from me or your Mom. Josh and I will have a discussion with your Mom about the information when she returns, but you being the oldest – it is your responsibility to make sure that whatever pact you and your brother make between one another that it is the right thing to do. Do you understand me?" said Tyrone sternly.

"Yes Daddy."

Alana and Josh never questioned anything Tyrone said to them. They knew their father meant business, and at no point were they allowed to try and argue their point. This time was certainly no different. As Josh made his way back to the table, he could see that Tyrone had that look on his face that clearly described the conversation he and Alana were having.

"Alright sweetheart, I love you and I am very proud of you. Please be safe and make good choices. Don't hesitate to call home if you need anything, OK," he said.

"Thank you, Daddy. I love you, too, and I promise to make good choices," she replied.

"Here's your bother."

Alana felt horrible, she knew she should have made Josh tell Sherita about the visit from the agents, but soon it will all be over and everything will be fine.

"Ok, big head, I love you. I will call you back in a couple of days when mom gets home," she said with a sigh.

"Ok – Sis. I love you, too. Be careful up there."

On the way home, Tyrone called a buddy of his who worked in the Fulton County District Attorney's office to see if he could get some more detailed information on Lamont. He learned that Lamont was facing federal charges of money laundering and that he was looking at doing a minimum of 10 years in prison. Because it was a federal case, the investigator didn't have much more information to provide. After they got in the house, Tyrone decided to give Kendra a call to see if she knew about Lamont's shady activity. If anybody could help break the news to Sherita about this situation, it would be Kendra.

"Hello," Kendra answered.

"Hey Kendra, its' Ty. You got a minute?"

"Ty, is everything OK? Wasn't expecting a call from you," Kendra said.

"Well, it appears as though our buddy Lamont is caught up in a federal money laundering investigation and the cops have been coming by the house looking for him.

"Shut the hell up! Tyrone are you serious?" Kendra yelled in complete shock.

"I knew that guy was a crook! There was always just something about him. What did Sherita say?" she asked.

"Well, that's just it. Sher doesn't know. Apparently the guys came to the house and spoke to Josh. Josh, in turn, called Lamont who indicated that he had everything under control and begged Josh not to tell his mom. However, Josh has been seeing guys staked out in cars in the neighborhood and decided to tell me tonight to figure out what to do. Kendra, Sherita will be home in a couple of days. According to my sources, this thing is about to hit the news really soon and Lamont's picture will be plastered everywhere. I think we need to break the news to Sherita first as soon as she lands before she sees it on TV or reads about it in the paper.

"I agree. It's funny, all this time she kept saying that Lamont had been acting weird the last few months, but she had been so preoccupied with everything else she just never got to the bottom of it," Kendra said.

"Yeah well, knowing Sherita the way that I do, she saw something in Lamont that no one else did to allow him into her world. And learning that he was involved in something this big will crush her. We have to have a plan, and it needs to be a good one."

Chapter 23

Sherita thought she was dreaming as she heard the light knock on her door. Having been there for nearly a week, she had gotten use to sleeping in late. As she rose up slightly, she focused to see Kroy standing at the door.

"Is everything alright," she asked as she wiped her eyes.

"Yes, Mi'Amore. Everything is fine," he whispered.

"Get dressed; I have something I want to show you. We will leave in about 20 minutes," he insisted.

"Dressed? Where are we going? What time is it," Sherita asked with a look of confusion on her face?

As she reached for her cellphone, she could see that it was 5:30 in the morning. Where could they possibly be going this early and what could he possibly have to show her that couldn't wait until daybreak? Her sleep felt good and she didn't want to interrupt that.

"Trust me; it will be well worth it. Now, come on get dressed. You can sleep in the car," he said with a sly smile on his face.

Sherita did as she was told and slowly got up and managed to get it together enough to meet the 20-minute deadline Kroy had placed upon their schedule. As they pulled out of the driveway, Sherita tried once more to find out where they were going.

"So, will you at least give me a hint as to where we are going," she asked with a playful tone?

"You are so cute," he said as he leaned over and kissed her on the cheek. "But, no. I am not going to give you a hint. Get comfortable and enjoy the ride. If you fall asleep I will wake you in time, I promise," he reassured her and headed toward the highway.

Sherita felt as though she had fallen asleep immediately. Her dreams were a historic reflection of the great people and food she had experienced so far on her trip. When she opened her eyes, she could see the break of dawn peeking through the clouds. They were traveling up an extremely steep mountaintop where the increasing level of elevation made her ears pop as if she were on an airplane. Watching Kroy driving on her right-hand side was very interesting to Sherita. She couldn't believe how comfortable she was with him. He was an amazingly passionate man and she even imagined exploring a greater relationship with him. While she sat and admired his beauty and daydreamed of the possibilities with him, she realized they were slowing down and coming to a stop. She sat up. "Mi'Amore," he said as he turned to face her.

"I need you to close your eyes and keep them closed until I tell you to open them. You are going to have to trust me, OK," he instructed.

"This is the first of a series of surprises I have, but you must participate and not waste any time."

Sherita agreed and closed her eyes and waited as Kroy came around the vehicle and gently helped her out of the car. The crispness of the morning air fought a valiant battle with the heated anticipation built up inside Sherita's body. While her eyes were closed, she could feel that they had gone from walking on concrete to what felt like a grassy wooded area. She could also sense that they were somehow standing at an angle, which lead to the thought of them being on a steep hill. The strong smell of fresh salt gave away the hint that they were definitely near water. "Few more steps Mi'Amore. You are doing great," he encouraged.

"Kroy, where are we?" Sherita asked with a twinge of excitement.

"Ok, when I count to three I want you to open your eyes and say the first thing that comes to mind," he said.

Kroy started counting.

"One."

He stood behind her and wrapped his arms around her pulling her close to him. "Two."

Sherita took in a deep breath at two wondering what it could be that was before her.

"Three!"

In that moment, Sherita stood speechless. In what appeared to be the perfect spot on this tremendous winding two-road mountain she stood staring at the most breath-taking view of the Atlantic Ocean. Even more amazing, Kroy had timed it perfectly to where she witnessed the awakening of the sun as it graced the earth with its powerful presence. The array of tropical wild flowers and exotic birds all managed to dance in a beautiful swirl of life taking on the dawn of a new day. As the sun claimed its place in the sky, the serene blue water met intricately with the lining of the sky to create an endless journey of peace. Kroy leaned into Sherita's ear.

"What do think Mi'Amore," he asked feeling good about his first fete.

"Oh my God. Kroy it is AMAZING. I mean, I am absolutely speechless. This is as close of a place to heaven on earth that I think I have ever seen," she said in awe.

Pulling her closer, he kissed her gently at the nape of her neck. He knew she would love it and was eager to get the rest of the day started so that he could continue to shower her with the simple beauties of his country and open his heart to show her how he felt. Having thought of everything, Kroy came prepared with a camera, because he knew Sherita would not want to miss this opportunity to capture the memory. Having anticipated this moment, Kroy programmed the camera to take a photo of the two of them together with the beautiful view in the background. As he set up his equipment, he hurried back over to pose with Sherita. Within a flash, the first of many memories was captured, with Kroy lovingly embracing Sherita from behind with the two of them smiling as though they were on their honeymoon. *Could it get any better than this?* Sherita thought to herself. Absolutely!

"Ok, Mi'Amore – on to the next surprise," Kroy said.

"What? There is more?" she said with excitement and smiling from ear-to-ear. "Yes, there is. Now get in the car," he insisted.

As they continued on their journey, Kroy reached over to sing along with the song playing on the radio. Blushing, Sherita immediately recognized the Caribbean artist Terrance Trent D'Arby as Kroy passionately took over the lead in singing the words to "Sign Your Name Across My Heart". This was truly going to be a great day. They rode for another half an hour to 45 minutes and all of a sudden approached the entrance to what appeared to be a beach. The sign up ahead read: Welcome to Las Cuevas Beach.

"Kroy, I am not dressed for the beach!" Sherita protested.

"Shhhh, Mi'Amore trust me, I have taken care of everything," he said in his normal calm tone of voice.

As they exited the car, Sherita could see the calm stillness of the white-sand beach with the amazingly blue water. Kroy took a single bag out of the trunk and grabbed Sherita by the hand. As he lead her down what seemed like a never-ending flight of stone-based stairs, Sherita could see in the distance two men. As they approached the men, it was apparent that they were preparing for what would be an intimate beach picnic for two. A luxurious white sheet covered a spot just under a large tree revealing hints of the sun. There was a picnic basket with an assortment of breakfast muffins, cheeses, juice, water and sandwiches for later in the day. There was a small transistor radio perched upon a ledge to prohibit its exposure to any blowing sand. Kroy reached in the bag that he had brought from the trunk and handed Sherita a beautiful earth-toned colored two-piece swimsuit. He directed her to the ladies shower room where she could change.

"Kroy, I am literally at a loss for words right now. I can't believe you have done all of this for me," she said with emotion in her voice.

"Mi'Amore, you deserve this and more and I want to be in a position to give you all that you need, want and desire," he said as he gazed into her eyes.

At that moment, Sherita couldn't help but think about Lamont. Although it was over between them, it had really only been a couple of months and she somehow felt bad about these extremely strong feelings she felt for Kroy. This week she had spent in Trinidad with him and his family was literally like no other experience she had ever had. She truly felt like a part of their family. It was just, so natural. "Listen, Kroy," she said as they sat Indian-style on the sheet.

"This entire week has truly been amazing and I promise you if not for my kids, I wouldn't leave in the next two days. I would stay and take it all in for as long as I could. But, I don't want to put myself in a position to where I am developing all of these feelings and go back to the United States and never hear from or see you again. I need a really clear understanding about your expectations. I just got out of a nearly yearlong relationship where I thought we were on the same page, but surprisingly we were literally on two different wavelengths. I don't want that with you," she said as she felt like she was rambling.

"Look, Sherita," he said with sincerity in his voice.

Sherita thought "*oh shit*" I ruined the day before it got started good, he hadn't called her by her name the entire time she had been there.

"I knew from the moment you walked through the doors at the hotel in Atlanta that you would be in my life. I knew because at that moment God spoke to me and said "*she is the one*". I didn't want to appear as though I was trying to make some corny move on you and I didn't want you to think I wasn't sincere in my efforts. So, I just let it work itself out in whatever way that God had in store for it to happen. I promise you, when I returned home from that weekend; I immediately started planning for this day right here, because I knew that I loved you and wanted to show you through my actions, not just through my words. So, all the other stuff that you've been through, I get that. I have been through some things as well, but God is giving you and me both an opportunity to start from here, together on a new journey. Just you and me," he said.

"Look," he continued. "Life is too short. You and I both have seen people we love and care about die too soon and not be able to experience in their lifetime even half of what we have experienced in these few days that you have been here with me. Don't focus on what can't be, focus on the reality of what is, and that is that you feel me as much as I feel you. Tell me I am wrong and I promise not to discuss it anymore today. We will just enjoy the view, the beach, the music and the company and head back to the city," he said during what appeared to be an ultimatum.

At this point, Sherita's hands were sweating. She really wanted to throw up that one church finger and excuse herself for a moment sneak off and call Kendra for direction on what to do. Everything Kroy was saying was true. Life was short and why not enjoy it to the fullest and let tomorrow worry about tomorrow.

"OK Kroy, what are you saying we should do?" she asked.

Kroy reached down into the bag and looked Sherita in her eyes.

"Accordez-vous une seconde chance a lamour et de choisir de m'aimer. Permettez-moi de vous honorer tous les jours de votre vie en acceptant d'etre mon espouse," he said.

It was the most beautiful flow of French Sherita had ever heard. Sitting in shock and amazement, she wasn't really sure what to say or how to respond.

"Huh?" she asked.

With a smile on his face, Kroy repeated himself as he pulled his hand from the bag revealing a brilliant cushion-cut diamond ring that sparkled against the reflection of the sun.

"Allow yourself a second chance at love and choose to love me. Allow me to honor you every day of your life, by agreeing to be my wife."

"*Oh shit,*" she thought. "*This dude is serious.*"

Chapter 24

Kendra snatched up the phone in hopes of hearing her best-friend's voice

on the other end. Sherita hadn't called since the first day saying she

arrived safely. She had only sent one email addressed to Kendra, Josh

and Alana nearly two days later saying she was having a great time and

that she would see everyone when she returned Sunday. Well, today was

the day that her friend was coming home and Kendra was anxious and

excited to hear about her trip and all the juicy details. Kendra and

Tyrone had agreed to both pick Sherita up at the airport. Tyrone had

called Kendra and gave her the update on the whole situation with

Lamont. They both agreed that it was best to just tell her, so that she

would know what to expect before she saw it on the news and went back

to work. Staring out the living room window waiting for Tyrone, Kendra

was distracted from her thoughts by the ringing of her cellphone.

"Hello, may I speak with Kendra," asked the woman on the other end of

the phone before Kendra could even speak.

"Yes, this is Kendra. How may I help you?" Kendra asked with a slight

attitude. "Yes, my name is Audra Washington, I am Lamont

Washington's ex-wife," she professed.

All of a sudden Kendra felt a sick-sinking feeling in her stomach. Why would Lamont's ex-wife be calling her and how did she get her number? "Ahhh, yes, how can I help you?" Kendra asked again with pouted lips and an attitude head role ready to snap.

"I have been trying to get in touch with Sherita for the past couple of days and I really need to speak with her. Do you know how I can reach her or can you have her give me a call," Audra asked.

"Ahh, she is out of the country. Is there something I can help you with? Is everything OK?" inquired Kendra as it sounded like she could hear sniffles on the other end of the phone.

Audra hesitated for a moment and with a deep sigh decided to share her information with Kendra.

"I don't know how to say this, but," she hesitated.

"Damn, say what? Spit it out already what is going on?" Kendra asked with frustration. "Where is Lamont? Is there something we should know?" she asked raising her voice.

"Yes. Lamont committed suicide two days ago," Audra, blurted out. The stillness of the room and the sudden silence in the phone gave Kendra the eerie feeling that the room was spinning.

"Excuse me," she managed to bring sound to the words she mouthed.

"His brother found him two days ago in his apartment. He left a note for me and our children and one for Sherita. I wanted to tell her first before she saw it on the news. The police don't suspect foul play, but giving the pending indictment that he was facing when he was scheduled to appear in court next week, they want to rule out all possibilities," Audra explained.

Kendra slowly reached for a chair at the kitchen table, ignoring the insistent car horn blowing from Tyrone in the driveway.

"Are you sure?" she asked Audra.

"Unfortunately, yes. I got Sherita's number off the front of the envelope he left for her. Please have her call me as soon as you speak with her. I don't know what went down with the two of them or why they broke up, but I do know that Lamont was very fond of Sherita and truly cared about her. So if you would please have her give me a call as soon as you speak with her, I don't want her to be caught off guard by this information," she said.

"Ahh, Ok, thank you. I will have her call you as soon as I reach her," Kendra hung up without saying goodbye.

She grabbed her jacket and headed to the car.

"Come on slow-poke you gone make us be stuck in traffic," Tyrone yelled out the car window.

Kendra got in the car in silence. She wasn't her usual quick-come-back sarcastic self with Tyrone. As they headed toward the airport, Tyrone realized something was either extremely wrong or Kendra was sick. She could never sit this long without talking.

"Hey. What's wrong with you?" Tyrone asked.

Scratching her head and taking a deep breath, Kendra said the words as if it were a dress rehearsal for how she would break the news to her friend. "Lamont committed suicide," she said calmly.

"What?" Tyrone said in disbelief.

"I was on the phone with his ex-wife when you pulled up. She was looking for Sherita to break the news to her. She said his brother found him two days ago in his apartment and he had left some handwritten notes for her, their twins and Sherita. Ty, how in the hell is she going to take this?" Kendra searched his face for the answer.

Tyrone took a deep breath. After the devastating loss of Allison only a couple of months ago, he knew that Sherita would be a wreck after receiving this type of news. Sherita wasn't a drama queen, so the news of the break-up between her and Lamont wasn't too shocking. Sherita was definitely one to walk away from something that didn't seem right. But she loved with her whole heart and once she cared about you, she truly cared about you. Sherita loved and cared for Lamont, so much so that she incorporated him into the lives of Alana and Josh. Tyrone braced himself to support his ex-wife's emotional state.

"Kendra, we just have to tell her," he said.

They rode in silence the rest of the way to the airport, each of them anticipating that it would be their responsibility to tell her the devastating news of Lamont's death. The two had already strategized about how they would tell her about the charges that were pending against him and about the encounter Josh had with the two federal agents. Their tag-team plan had been destroyed right before their eyes and now they both had to prepare themselves for an even greater bombshell. As they pulled into the airport parking garage Tyrone's cellphone started ringing. It was Josh.

"Dad!" he said anxiously.

"I just saw a report on the news saying that Lamont Washington was found dead in his apartment as a result of an apparent suicide! Dad is it true?" Josh asked with grave concern.

"Yes son, I am afraid so. Aunt Kendra and I just heard," Tyrone said calmly.

"Oh my God Dad, Mom is going to be devastated. Does she know yet? Have you guys picked her up?" he asked.

"No son, we are just parking the car now and headed in to meet your Mom at baggage claim. Don't worry son, everything is going to be OK. We will see you when we get to the house," Tyrone assured his son.

"Ok dad. Are you guys going to tell her when you see her?" Josh asked. He felt hopeless and really didn't want his mom to be hurt.

"Probably," Tyrone said.

Kendra and Tyrone stood nervously near the baggage claim portal waiting for Sherita.

"HELLO," Sherita shrieked as she came around the corner with a burst of excitement and arms outstretched!

Smiling from ear-to-ear Sherita had a fabulous tan and literally had the most amazing glow and look of relaxation. She looked extremely happy.

"Well who would've thought that you two would ever fight over who would pick me up from the airport," she said jokingly.

"Clearly you guys rode in separate cars, right?" she said laughing out loud.

Trying to be as normal as possible, neither Kendra nor Tyrone had much to say. The scene was playing out like the end to a bad love story where at the climax just when you think the girl will get her prince something bad happens. As the three stood waiting for the bags to circle their way around the carousel, Tyrone and Kendra glanced nervously at one another. Sherita talked a mile a minute, completely oblivious to the unusual silence between Ty and Kendra.

"Uhm, Sher, how was your trip?" Kendra asked.

"Guys, it was AMAZING," Sherita said with stars in her eyes.

"I can't wait to tell you all about it. And I have some really interesting and exciting news that is truly going to blow you away," she continued to ramble on and on.

"Sher, how many bags do you have?" Tyrone asked.

"There are two that we are waiting on. Hopefully, they will be up soon," she said. "What is going on with you two? Did you guys have a fight on the way to the airport?"

"No, we didn't fight Sher. Here, let's sit down over here while we wait for the bags to come up," suggested Tyrone.

Kendra immediately took him up on the offer and sat in the first seat.

"Seriously, Ty? I have been sitting on an airplane nonstop for the past four hours and you want me to sit? What is going on?" she asked again, now with real concern.

"Sherita, I got a call earlier today saying that Lamont committed suicide," Kendra blurted out before she knew it.

With a look of confusion and bewilderment, Sherita shook her head lightly and asked her friend to repeat what she said.

"Excuse me?" She asked.

"Sher, it's true. Lamont is dead," Tyrone confirmed.

Feeling lightheaded, hot and sweaty, Sherita looked into Tyrone's eyes in search of understanding. As she attempted to make sense of it all, she could feel herself losing control of her body. With quick reaction, Tyrone caught Sherita's limp body just before she hit the floor. Kendra jumped up immediately screaming Sherita's name and looking around for some help.

"Oh my God, SHERITA!" she screamed.

"Someone call 911," yelled Tyrone.

As he fell to the floor, bracing her body against his, Tyrone tried intently to snap Sherita back into consciousness.

"Sherita. Baby. Talk to me," he said with exasperation as he patted her face seeking a reaction.

Nearby airport security officers ran over to lend a hand during the commotion. A Delta reservation agent rushed over with paper towels and a bottle of water. Tyrone continued to call out Sherita's name.

"Sherita! Sherita, wake up baby," he repeated.

"What happened?" inquired one of the guards.

"She fainted. We had to deliver some disturbing news and she just didn't react in the manner we had planned," explained Kendra.

Sprinkling spurts of water on her face, Tyrone continued to call out to Sherita to regain consciousness all the while rocking her back and forth. The commotion was creating a crowd of on-lookers. Within a couple of minutes, Sherita began to come around. She could hear the muffled sounds of people around her and was a bit dazed when she initially came to.

"What happened?" she asked as she attempted to sit up holding her head.

"You fainted," Tyrone said.

As she looked up into Tyrone's face and looked around she made eye contact with Kendra who stood with tears in her eyes. Sherita knew then that the news she received moments earlier was in fact true. Lamont was dead. As she rested her head in Tyrone's chest, Sherita sobbed out loud with cries of hurt, pain and anguish.

"No! No! Why God Why?" She sobbed. He was gone. He was really gone.

Chapter 25

Sherita was nervous as she dialed Audra's number. Up until this point, she had never formally met her in person. Their interactions had been very limited to Sherita staying in the car on the days when Lamont would pick up the twins. "Hello," said the voice on the other end of the phone solemnly.

"Um, yes, may I speak with Audra please?" Sherita asked.

"Yeah, this is Audra. Who is this?" she said dryly.

"Audra, this is Sherita. Sherita Coleman," she repeated.

There was about five seconds of silence in the phone that seemed endless. "Sherita, thanks for calling. I assume that by now your girlfriend has shared with you the news regarding Lamont?" Audra asked.

"Ah, yes. I...," Sherita replied fighting back tears.

With a heavy sigh she says, "yes, I know." "What happened?" Sherita asked with confusion.

"Well, apparently this recent bout of legal troubles that Lamont, and his partner have gotten themselves into was going to result in hard time in federal prison. I guess he didn't want to face that," Audra said non-chalantly.

"Prison?" Sherita said overwhelmed.

"I had no idea that any of this was going on. When did all of this start?" Sherita started spewing questions at Audra as if she were interviewing her for a television exclusive. Her thoughts were swirling around in her head to the events of the past six months with Lamont and how secretive he had become and then the multiple random phone calls. She just didn't give any thought to the fact that anything this serious could be going on and especially not to the point of prison or death. "Look, Sherita, I would say I am sorry for your loss, but given the fact that you two weren't even together I am surprised that you even care," Audra said matter-of-factly.

"What do you mean?" Sherita replied with offense in her voice.

"Lamont and I were together for a very long time and grew to care about one another deeply. Now while I was not aware of every little thing he was involved in, I certainly would never want to see anything bad happen to him and especially something like this," she defended.

"Yeah, well, Lamont had a knack for being secretive," Audra replied coyly. "Look, Audra. I don't know you and it is obvious that you don't know me and quite frankly I am OK with that. But the fact of the matter is Lamont is dead and you and I are in a very unique situation to have to deal with this horrible reality. Now, I am just attempting to show you some compassion seeing as how you are the mother of his children, and this has to be a difficult position for you. So, this non-chalant, kiss-my-ass attitude you have you can save that shit because right now nobody gives a damn!"

Sherita could feel her heart rate increase and tried desperately to regain control of her emotions. The intent of this call was not to have an attitude battle with Lamont's ex-wife she just wanted to offer her condolences and her support.

"You're right," Audra said with a sigh. "It has been a rough couple of days for me."

"And what, you think I been over here planting pansies or something?" Sherita was heated.

"Yo! Slow it down honey!" Audra said with a raised voice.

Realizing that both of them had the capacity to go from 0 to 10 immediately, Audra thought she'd better change the tone of the conversation quick.

"Listen, Sherita, even though you and Lamont were no longer a couple, it is obvious that you guys cared a lot about one another. Therefore, I would appreciate you and your kids being at the services. I have scheduled everything for next Tuesday at 1:00 p.m. at the New Macedonia Baptist Church downtown. If it is OK with you, I would like for the two of us to somehow help each other through it." Sherita suddenly felt sorry for Audra. She couldn't imagine what she must be going through having to plan a funeral for her children's father given their once tumultuous relationship. She didn't know what she would do if anything ever happened to Tyrone. The thought gave her chill bumps.

"Thank you. My family and I will be there to support you and your children through this difficult situation. Please let me know if there is anything I can do to help you."

"Thank you Sherita. I appreciate that. If you would, please be here at noon to ride in the family car with us. I think Lamont would have wanted that."

Pleasantly surprised at Audra's sudden change in tone, Sherita accepted

the invitation and grabbed a pen and paper to take down the address

information. Once the call ended, Sherita sat in silence for about 15

minutes just trying to make sense of it all. She really did care deeply for

Lamont and hated to know that she would never speak with him again.

She felt saddened by the thought. With mixed emotions about it all, she

also couldn't stop thinking about Kroy. She hadn't had an opportunity to

share with her kids the news and now with all of this she wasn't quite

sure how they would take it. She needed to hear Kroy's voice, so she

called. Sherita found herself day-dreaming and intrigued at the sound of

the foreign dial tone. She almost forgot that she had dialed the number,

as it seemed as though it had rung a hundred times.

"Good Day!" Kroy answered sounding out of breath.

"Hi sweetie, it's me," Sherita said calmly.

"Ahhh…Mi'Amore, how are you?" he said with a smile.

"Um, I'm OK. Did I disturb you?"

"No, no. Not at all, I was just finishing up my workout here in the gym,

but I am always happy to stop and speak with you," he said. "Is

everything OK? You sound funny."

218

Sherita took a deep breath and closed her eyes as they filled with tears. She was still in disbelief but needed to share her feelings with someone.

"Um. When I got home yesterday, my ex-husband Tyrone and my best friend Kendra came to pick me up from the airport. I didn't think anything of it, I was just still reeling over my high from my time there in Trinidad with you and looking forward to sharing with them my amazing news," she paused to hold back her tears.

"Yeah, what happened?" he asked calmly.

"They informed me that Lamont was found dead in his apartment a couple of days ago. Apparently he killed himself."

Sherita sobbed lightly as she searched the top of the nightstand for some tissue. Unsuccessful, she grabbed one of Josh's T-shirts off the nearby lounge chair.

"Oh my God! Mi'Amore, I am so very sorry to hear that. Do they know why? Did you have any indication that he was disturbed by anything that would lead to this outcome?" he questioned one by one.

"No! Apparently he was in some sort of legal trouble that was going to land him in federal prison for a very long time and he just couldn't deal with the thought of doing time. I am just out done by it all and just really

not sure what to think." Sherita said.

"So, what happens next?" he asked.

"Well, I spoke with his ex-wife just before I called you and she gave me

the information for the services next Tuesday at 1 p.m. She asked if me

and the kids would come and ride in the family car to the funeral.

Sweetie, I am just so overwhelmed."

"I know Mi'Amore. I know. I wish I was there with you to hug you

right now. It is an unfortunate turn of events that you have reported back

to, but you will make it through this. I promise."

"Thank you, sweetie, I wish you were here, too."

Sherita felt relieved talking to Kroy. He really was special. His kind

demeanor and supportive nature was going to be a welcomed aspect in

her life. The two chatted a bit longer, discussing the logistics of how and

when Sherita would share their news with her family. As she listened,

his island accent sounded like a well-produced musical track. She smiled

at the fact that during her vacation she managed to understand every

word he said. Although she was sad about Lamont, Sherita was happy

about the possibility of the future.

Chapter 26

The ride in the limo to the church was surreal. Sherita had been numb ever since she got the news of Lamont's death. It was all just so unreal, she couldn't believe that all this time Lamont had been dealing with this craziness and didn't think he could share it with her. Sherita was angry with him that he would be such a coward about it and take his own life. She wished she could've done something, anything, but instead she was left with more unanswered questions and yet another funeral. The church was packed with wall-to-wall people. There were news cameras everywhere and Sherita thought this entire seen was unbelievable. Kendra and the kids rode with her in the limo with Audra and the twins, and Tyrone and Nicole followed close behind.

"I will be glad when this is all over, maybe then, we can finally get on with our life," Nicole said sarcastically under her breath.

"Honey, I know this has been a lot to deal with the past few weeks, but what else did you expect me to do? She is my ex-wife and the mother of my kids. I don't want to see them hurt. I just want to make sure they are OK," Tyrone said with a sigh.

"Ty, I understand you being there for your kids, but you said so yourself, she is your 'EX-WIFE!'"

she replied as she rolled her eyes and looked out the window at the large crowd outside the church. The past few months had been unnerving for Nicole. Tyrone had somehow decided that it was his responsibility to help see Sherita through this entire ordeal. Although she didn't have any issues with Sherita, she was getting tired of her man constantly running to save the day. She had tried her best to be patient through all of this, but honestly it was getting on her last nerve.

Sherita replayed the discussion with Audra in her head as she walked in what seemed like slow motion down the aisle. Audra later shared that, early on in their marriage Lamont had become mixed up in a robbery scheme with some guys he grew up with and as a result he spent the first two years of their relationship in prison. Lamont had never mentioned that he had been in that type of trouble, though, Sherita never asked either. Realizing what lies ahead for her future, she knew that she would need to do a little more digging. Blindsided by the news of Lamont's passing at the airport, Sherita hadn't shared the news with her kids about her pending engagement to Kroy. She felt so connected to him and almost couldn't believe herself that she was about to marry a man she

had only known for such a short time. Kroy and his family made her feel

at home and everything in her told her this was the right thing to do. She

just hoped that her kids would be receptive to it all. She missed Kroy

and really wished he could be there with her now, but she didn't think it

would be fair or appropriate to ask him to accompany her to the funeral

of her ex-lover.

"Lord my life," she thought. As she snapped back to reality, the loud

music broke her concentration, and Sherita and Audra supported each

other down the aisle, linked arm and arm, holding onto separate

memories of a man they both loved and cherished. Because of the

extensive damage, Audra had elected for a closed casket. It was for the

best, Sherita thought it made sense for Lamont's family and friends to

remember him as the loving and kind person that he was and not allow

their last image of him to be laying in a coffin. As the crowd continued

to file into the church, the choir sang a soulful rendition of 'Goin Up

Yonder'. When she looked around, Sherita couldn't help but wonder

who all these people were? She barely recognized any of them.

"Good afternoon church. You may be seated," Reverend Hinton said.

"We are here today for the home going celebration of Mr. Lamont Stephen Washington. We will follow the schedule within the program that you have before you. I would ask, however, at this time that out of respect that you please turn off your cellphones and any other devices. It is my understanding that there are news cameras outside the church waiting to get any information that they can, pertaining to the services. I would also ask, that each of you honor this family's wishes and elect not to involve yourselves in any opportunity to share anything about this service. This is God's house, and we will respect God's rules. Now with that being said, Minister Tom Hillshire will come and read a scripture from the Old Testament, followed by Minister Corey Dewberry who will read from the New Testament. Please let us receive them in that order."

Josh and Alana sat behind their mom with feelings of helplessness. Sherita had been very quiet and distant in the days since learning of Lamont's death. As news continued to be released through the media there continued to be much speculation surrounding Lamont's involvement with the federal case and also strong allegations of an international drug trade ring. Sherita refused to believe that Lamont had anything to do with such outlandish stories. She recounted over and over again in her head the times he would be on the phone trying to remember anything about any of those conversations. The federal authorities had questioned her and her kids extensively, as they still had a case pending against Lamont's business partner Chris. Unfortunately, there just wasn't much that Sherita could share with them. Lamont and Sherita never discussed work at home. She was just as much in the dark as they were.

"Our old testament scripture will come from Psalms 23:1-6. If you have your Bibles, please read along silently. I will be reading from the New International Version. *The Lord is my shepherd, I lack nothing. He makes me lie down in green pastures, he leads me beside quiet waters, he refreshes my soul. He guides me along the right paths for his name's sake. Even though I walk through the darkest valley, I will fear no evil, for you are with me, your rod and your staff, they comfort me. You prepare a table before me in the presence of my enemies. You anoint my head with oil; my cup overflows. Surely your goodness and love will follow me all the days of my life, and I will dwell in the house of the Lord forever.*"

Minister Hillshire read the scripture with so much fervor that many of those in the room clapped boldly in a show of support and agreement. Kendra was getting antsy. She wasn't a big fan of funerals and she was worried about Sherita and how she was really holding up. She got up and politely excused herself to go to the restroom. While she stood in the vestibule waiting to re-enter the service, she noticed Kroy and an older woman entering the church.

"Kroy?" she called out.

Kroy reached out to shake Kendra's hand, vaguely remembering her face from the hotel when he first met Sherita.

"Hello," he said.

"I am Kendra, Sherita's best friend. We met at the Ritz Carlton," she explained. "Oh, yes, yes, yes Kendra! How are you? Thank you so much for reminding me." He replied as he simultaneously helped the older woman inside.

"This is my mother, Auhna LaBeauf. We just landed and hoped to make it in time for the services," he said.

The two women shook hands and Kendra smiled pleasantly. She could see where Kroy got his strikingly good looks from, his mother was beautiful.

"Wow, that was sweet of you to come. You haven't missed too much and I am sure Sherita will be glad to see you. It's been tough for her over the past few days, but she is holding up." Kendra said.

"Good. Well I am here to show my support," he said.

As they all waited for an opportunity to enter the sanctuary, Kendra remembered that in the midst of all the hustle and bustle since Sherita had been back, she hadn't had a chance to inquire about her trip. Sherita seemed extremely excited to share some news at the airport and Kendra needed to get the scoop.

Following the services, Sherita was glad to see Kroy and his mom. She really missed him and was pleasantly surprised that he would show such a great level of support. She knew deep down that she cared a lot for Lamont, but there was something about Kroy that she loved. Yet, she had butterflies in her stomach as to what Josh and Alana's reaction will be to her agreeing to marry him. She intended to make peace with Lamont's passing and was determined to focus on the good times with him. After a long conversation with Audra, she realized that Lamont had been anxiously trying to clear up his legal woes for several years, long before Sherita came into the picture. Knowing that there was nothing she could do about it now, Sherita decided to move forward with her life. And that life would include Kroy. Kendra stopped by Sherita's house the next day to check on her to see how she was doing and to see Alana before Tyrone took her to the airport. While Sherita sat daydreaming about the life yet to come, her concentration was broken by a knock at the door.

"Hey girl, I was just thinking about you," Sherita said as Kendra entered the kitchen.

"Why what's up?"

Sherita thought now was as good a time as any to share her news with her family before Alana headed back to New York. She didn't think it would be fair to share such big news over the phone. With Kendra, Josh and Alana sitting around the table, she knew she needed to talk fast before Kroy and Auhna arrived for the formal introductions.

"Ok guys. First let me say, thank you to each of you for all the love and support you all have shown me over the past few days and months with everything that has been going on. Who would have thought, that our lives would be turned so upside down within such a short amount of time. I know I have been a little wacky, but I assure you I am OK and on the road back to normalcy," she laughed.

"Yeah, well we still need to hear about this trip to Trinidad," Kendra said slyly. "Yeah, Ma! How was your trip? Did you bring a brotha anything back?" Josh asked jokingly.

"Well, my trip was pretty exciting. Trinidad is very beautiful."

"Yeah, yeah, yeah chick get to the good stuff, we don't want to hear that hallmark shit," Kendra insisted.

"Ok. Guys, I said yes," Sherita blurted out with excitement and a huge smile on her face.

"Wait. What?" Alana said while looking confused.

"Said yes to what?" Josh asked with an attitude.

Glancing at her friends' hand, Kendra immediately noticed a bright new big and shiny rock on Sherita's ring finger.

"Oh my God! Oh my God! Oh my God!" Kendra screamed out loud jumping up and down and hugging Sherita with joy.

"Josh, Lan – Mommy is getting married! Surprise!?" she tried to ease the words out of her mouth in a way that her kids would be excited, but it didn't seem to be working.

Just as Sherita was about to explain to her family the news the doorbell rang. "Wait! Mom! Do you think this is such a good idea?" Josh asked as she opened the door for Kroy and Auhna.

It was all too much for Alana to understand. She sat down at the kitchen table with tears in her eyes and in shock. She wanted to be excited for her mom, but given all that had just taken place with this whole Lamont situation, she just didn't know what to think. Could her mom really be serious?

"Everyone, I would like you to meet Kroy LaBeauf my fiancé," Sherita said with excitement.

"Kroy, I would like you to meet my kids Josh and Alana."

"Hi guys. Judging by the looks on your faces, I will assume your mother just told you about our engagement," Kroy said a bit disturbed at this revelation.

Clapping and smiling, Kendra is singing "happy, happy, joy, joy," trying desperately to lighten the mood in the room.

Not feeling it at all, Josh is pissed. With a look of anger and a strong sense of protection, he looked at Kroy and said, "Dude, I don't know what she told you, but you ain't marrying my Momma," as he refused to shake Kroy's extended hand.

Josh then abruptly pushed his way past Kroy and Auhna and headed down the hall to his room and slammed the door.

"JOSH!" Sherita yelled in shock at her son's reaction. She knew he would not be thrilled over it, but she certainly did not expect such a rude outburst.

"It's OK Mi'Amore. He is in shock," Kroy said.

Alana walked over to shake Kroy's hand and give a hug to Auhna.

"Nice to meet you both," she said nervously.

"Hopefully your brother will come around, we are looking forward to having you all become a part of our family," Auhna said.

Looking over at Sherita with uncertainty, Alana shook her head in confusion and headed down the hall after her brother. While silence fell over the room, Sherita looked over at Kendra for some level of support.

"Don't look at me, sweetie. You baked this cake!" she said as she sat down.

Sherita quickly realized that this whole thing did not go as she had imagined. She knew that the surprise of all of this would shock her kids. It just felt right and she knew that once Josh got to know Kroy he would learn to love him, just as she did. After all, with everything she had been through, she realized her normal life had become anything but normal.

Tracye D. Bryant

In Loving Memory of...

Thaddeus "Lamar" Corbin
June 27, 1970 – May 11, 2011

Tanya Stone
March 27, 1967 – April 30, 2003

The two of you loved and supported me unconditionally and believed in me even when there were times that I didn't believe in myself. The impact that each of you have made in my life will never be forgotten. Thank you for being my Guardian Angels in heaven reminding each day that I am a "soldier" who has nothing to worry about, because I will be taken care of for the rest of my life. May you both Rest in Peace. Save me a seat in heaven.

"To live in hearts we leave behind is not to die"~ Thomas Campbell, poet.